Simply Living

Simply Living was produced in association with the Center for World Indigenous Studies and the Endangered People's Project. A portion of the royalties from *Simply Living* will aid these groups.

Simply Living

The Spirit of the
Indigenous People

Edited by Shirley Ann Jones

Preface by Dr. Rudolph Ryser
Foreword by Brooke Medicine Eagle
Afterword by Mutang Urud

New World Library
Novato, California

New World Library
14 Pamaron Way
Novato, California 94949

Copyright © 1999 by Shirley Ann Jones

Cover design: Alexandra Honig
Cover photograph: Phil Borges / Two women from Turkana tribe in Baragoi, Kenya
Text design: Jason Gardner
Illustrations based on indigenous designs: Denise Gardner

Library of Congress Cataloging-in-Publication Data
Simply Living : the spirit of the indigenous people / edited by
   Shirley Jones.
   p. cm.
ISBN 1-57731-054-3 (alk. paper)
1. Ethnophilosophy. 2. Indigenous peoples Quotations. I. Jones,
   Shirley A., 1947–
GN468. 56   1999
306 .08—dc21

99-28616
CIP

First printing, August 1999
ISBN 1-57731-054-3
Printed in Canada on acid-free, recycled paper
Distributed to the trade by Publishers Group West

10 9 8 7 6 5 4 3

CONTENTS

PREFACE

Wisdom, we usually think, originates with our ancestors. We turn to them for the comfort and security of ideas tested over time. In wisdom we glimpse truth. We all recognize truth in the simple, the unadorned, the direct, and the uncomplicated. This is the experience of all people in all places throughout the world. The wise among us know and understand these things to be self-evident.

I have the pleasure of drawing your attention, your mind and person, to this wonderful collection of thoughts from the far reaches of the earth — everywhere human beings have explored and become a part of the natural surroundings. Friends of mine speak many of the words you will read. Other voices come from lands I have visited. They come from nations that work to defend themselves against encroachments by outside development or by violent wars aimed at destroying the people. The words you read are from Fourth World peoples who are simply living their lives.

The words "native" or "indigenous" have become popular ways of talking about peoples who live in Fourth World nations. Neither of these words, however, reaches the depth of meaning or precision of the word "people." This one word is translated or translatable into every human language.

The words for "people" around the world are so beautiful they sing. Listen as you say Inuit (IN uu EET), Naga (NAA gaa), Lakota, Hopi, Yanomami (YAA no MOMee), Ainu (EYE new), Mong, Palua (baa LOW), Karimojong, Dogon (DOE gone), Yup'ik, and Taidnapum (ti ID NAA pum). By these words and thousands more spoken in more than six thousand languages, we immediately recognize the richness of human diversity joined by common knowledge.

The Hopi, Maya, Cowlitz, Maori, and many other peoples tell the story of their origins. Often these stories place the human being among plants, animals, mountains, oceans, wind, land, and sky, as the youngest being of them all. The human being was given a brain not to dominate and control all things but instead to learn everything necessary to survive and live. All other things in the world already possess, say the stories, the essential knowledge of existence. As the youngest of all beings, humans would learn from the plants, other animals, mountains, oceans, wind, land, sky, and all other things. Indeed, the human's greatest duty was, and is, to learn respect for these things so that people can live and survive. To fail this simple duty means humans suffer and, at long last, will be destroyed by forces of their own making.

Using their brain to learn, humans make their individual cultures different and distinct. By molding to their environments, cultures ensure human survival in each of the thousands of places people live. Each culture is an evolved and dynamic relationship between humans, the earth, and the cosmos. This relationship provides many different methods of trading; making clothes; practicing politics; experiencing religion; practicing social customs; exploiting earth for food, shelter, and garments; entertaining; and creating bonds through ritual, dance, song, and other fine arts.

Diverse cultures provide a rich reservoir of knowledge and experience to enrich the human experience. That there are so many cultures in the world stands as strong testimony of how successful humans have been learning from the earth, the plants, the other animals, and the sky.

As the editor of this fine book points out, all human beings on the earth have a connection to Fourth World peoples — the original peoples. Many of the world's thousands of nations persist today, although few human beings remain connected to their original peoples. From the time humans began, they migrated from one territory to another. And inevitably some settled in areas overlapping with other settled peoples. This process of migration and change was slow. In only the recent past, the last four or five hundred years, has the slow pace of millennia begun to accelerate with the new speed that larger human populations could achieve. For the first time in history, certain populations regularly traveled around the world and began to settle where other humans had settled thousands of years earlier. Previously, there had been some overlapping settlement of territories in what are now the states of Iraq and Iran, and even resettlement of lands already occupied in Europe and Asia forty thousand years ago, but not until the recent past have humans begun to regularly circumnavigate the world, introducing rapid social and economic change to long-settled communities.

This relatively recent phenomenon of human contact and settlement all around the world certainly has resulted in dramatic change for many peoples. Population migrations have also meant something else: people rejecting and then forgetting their connection to ancient cultures.

What is now called "disconnection" — the psychological notion that people suffer from socially, emotionally, and even politically distancing themselves from their cultural roots — torments many who know they suffer and many millions more who don't comprehend the concept. This disconnection contributes to a growing gap between the citizen-consumers of the world and the keepers of ancient human knowledge.

In an age when most people live in cities, only small minorities actually have direct access to the earth — to the earth's rhythms of life. Lacking this access to earth's rhythmic reality, growing numbers of people are losing touch with simple human experiences. Cities, each with tens of millions of citizens, speckle the earth's surface, creating the illusion of global overpopulation. Densely populated modern cities, filled with commerce and information, act like giant amoebas consuming all of the environment's nutrients, while thousands of tiny, diverse cultural communities — Fourth World peoples — strive to survive by balancing their needs against the capacity of the earth's natural ability to regenerate. As the polarity intensifies between massive cities and their reliance on consumerism and the thousands of small, culturally distinct people (relying on self-controlled production), pressures increase in the cities to swallow-up what I call the "wild seed of humanity."

The ability of Fourth World people to "keep their feet on the ground" gives them knowledge about the earth and her rhythms — information required to remain human — that is only hinted at in the city citizen's realm of knowledge. To comprehend this knowledge, citizens have to reclaim their identity, their connection to their many cultures and to the earth. Instead of merely consuming the knowledge of humanities' wild seed, each individual must relearn earth's rhythms and celebrate human diversity. The Fourth World peoples hold great wisdom and great benefit comes from knowing what is true. Those who possess this wisdom will share it on their terms; it is on this basis that relearning can occur.

When the last great effort to extract knowledge from the world's native peoples began in the late-fifteenth century, colonizers showed a great desire to take and wantonly destroy with little under-standing of what was at stake. Now, as the twenty-first century begins, we're experiencing a similar inclination to "prospect" what remains of the world's diversity and convert it into consumer prod-ucts. We don't need to take this course. The world's Fourth World peoples have a simple message for their brothers and sisters living in consumer societies. Some of that message and rich knowledge you hold in your hands. Begin now to respect and relearn what your ancestors knew and what some of your elders know still.

— DR. RUDOLPH RŸSER

About Dr. Rÿser

Dr. Rudolph C. Rÿser is the founder and chair of the Center for World Indigenous Studies. He is a member of the Cowlitz Indian Tribe. His family comes from the headwaters of the Cowlitz River where his mother Ruth was born and where the northern Cowlitz, known as the Taidnapum, live. Most of the 4,500 or so Cowlitz live in and round the Cowlitz River west of the Cascade Mountain spine in what is now called southwest Washington State in the United States. His father, Ernest, comes from an ancient family called "Rÿser" — meaning "forest keeper" — located in the mountains to the northeast of Bern, Switzerland, in the town called Burgdorf. Nearly all of the 7,500 or so "Rÿsers" live in and around Burgdorf. Dr. Rÿser is a pro-fessor of International Relations, teaching Fourth World Geopolitics at the Center for World Indigenous Studies Learning Retreat, Xipe Totec (from the Nauhtl for "God of Renewal"). Dr. Rÿser is the father of three sons, Christian, Jon, and Morgan. He lives with his wife, Dr. Leslie Korn, in a small village in western Mexico.

About the Center for World Indigenous Studies

The Center for World Indigenous Studies is an independent, non-governmental research and education organization established in 1984 to advance the knowledge and ideas of Fourth World peoples and to promote constructive dialogue between Fourth World peoples and peoples of metropolitan states. The Center is organized on the following principle: Access to knowledge and peoples' ideas reduces the possibility of conflict and increases the possibility of cooperation between peoples on the basis of mutual consent. By democratizing relations between peoples, between nations and states, the diversity of nations and their cultures will continue to enrich the world. The Center for World Indigenous Studies offers professional development seminars, certifications and master's degrees in Fourth World studies, and traditional medicine through its Fourth World Institute and the Center for Traditional Medicine. CWIS also conducts a conflict management program, an extensive research program, and publishes monographs and the *Fourth World Journal*. Their website is www.cwis.org.

FOREWORD

I am proud to introduce this book of global native wisdom. I have known Shirley, who compiled these wonderful words, since a trip in the Yucatan Peninsula of Mexico she and her husband joined many years ago. We have since become close friends, and I am always inspired by the depth of her own wisdom and caring, which is reflected in this very special book.

I have attempted to live my life as a demonstration that the wisdom of my native ancestors will work in the modern world. It has become clear to me that it not only works, it is vitally necessary. As we face the challenges of the disharmony we've created for ourselves, we must regain this ancient and everlasting wisdom in order to create solutions that truly work for us, the larger family of life around us, and for seven generations of children.

Living this wisdom can bring us home and help us return to a sense of belonging where we learn to own things with our love and commitment instead of paper and money. In the old days, you "owned" what you could care for and relate to from your heart. Too often these days we buy what we think we want, yet we have no time for relationship with it, whether it is a beautiful piece of land or a sacred object.

I like to think about the young boy who wanted a special ceremonial rattle like his grandfather's, so his grandfather said, "You shall have one." It was winter and nothing was mentioned again. The boy respectfully waited. When the spring winds began to blow and thaw the frozen ground, Grandfather took him to one of the crop storage cellars, and they examined handfuls of gourd seeds. He let the boy pick the number that would fit in his small hand and put them in a special pouch. The boy understood then that he would be growing the gourd that would make his rattle. Planting the seeds in the sweet-smelling ground, tending the tiny shoots as they burst forth and became viney plants, carrying water to them when the late summer brought dry weather, praying over them, telling them about the life they would lead as rattles for his people — these things were a joy and a deep lesson to the boy.

At last the gourds were grown and ready to dry. He picked them and hung them on a shady porch, going by often to touch them. One seemed to call to him, and he finally chose it from the array of beautiful gourds. Then Grandfather and he went searching for a handle. They went down by the river where the water had washed many broken branches to shore and chose one that perfectly fit his hand; they would never have cut a living branch when it was possible to find one like this.

As the autumn came, so came the day when the boy and his grandfather sat down with the beautiful gourd, prayed and gave thanks for the plants which gave them these gifts, and began the construction. The boy was so excited that he scraped too hard when cleaning out the seeds and broke through the wall of the gourd! Oh, he cried and cried. His grandfather simply helped him lay that one aside and begin the process of choosing again. This time they knew to look for one that was sturdy and thick as well as attractive. He took great care, and finally the gourd was ready to be dried. They went and buried the remains of both gourds with prayers of thanksgiving.

Then Grandfather told the boy to run and find a cricket to help the rattle learn how to sing. It took him most of two days, but he came back at last with one gently held between his two hands. They put it in the now-dry gourd; it sang and sang as the evening light came over the village. The boy knew his rattle would be a good singer, too. The next morning he went to find small stones, asking the ant people who gathered them to give him a few, and giving them seeds as a gift in return. Grandfather gifted him with sinew, saying that someday he would learn to hunt for himself the deer that provided it. "I want something of mine to go with you in the rattle, anyhow," Grandfather said with a kind smile.

So they completed the rattle, and the boy took the cricket back to where he had found him and sang him a special song as he hopped away. Then the boy spent a day sitting alone on a high hill to become well acquainted with his new rattle. That year, he danced for the first time in the autumn dances of thanksgiving for all the gifts that graced his people's lives. He now knew more about owning something with his love. So, later, when his younger sister admired his rattle and wanted one, the boy completed the giveaway cycle by taking her the next spring into the storage cellar to pick out her own gourd seeds. Grandfather proudly came along.

In another time and place, a young boy saw a ceremonial rattle in the window of a store and wanted it. Because his father had the money to buy it, the boy received it for his birthday. The boy shook it and played with it for awhile, but eventually it ended up gathering dust on a shelf in his room.

The difference in these ways of being and living, of acquiring things, has so many lessons for us. Those lessons are about quality and communion versus quantity, about relationship versus ownership. They allow us to see what truly makes us happy. The native boy developed his relationship not only with the gourd, but with his grandfather, the land, the creatures, the seasonal cycles, the ways of the craftsman, and with the ceremonial life of his people. It gave him a sense of belonging to the place and the larger life around him; it gave him a sense of his own capability; it gave him gifts that cannot be bought, which he in turn gave away.

Simply Living has many gifts like this for all of us in this modern day if we take them to heart and put them into practice in our own lives. I commend to you their lovely and beneficial words.

— BROOKE MEDICINE EAGLE
Lakota/Crow, Scot/Irish

INTRODUCTION

The term "indigenous" requires no introduction. That is the very nature of the word. When something is "indigenous" to an area, a land, a continent, a country, a region, an environment, it inherently has the quality of not being introduced from the outside. It needs no "look here" because it is already there, firmly rooted.

Indigenous peoples have lived on the lands of their ancestors since the beginning of history. They are progeny of the original inhabitants. They are native, belonging naturally to the soil and land, living in balance with their environment.

The indigenous peoples in *Simply Living* do not need to call attention to their words; their lives speak for themselves. Most are rooted in seven generations of land and culture. Many have traveled into the modern world, moving from place to place, yet always carrying inside their innate being. They all speak out individually as members of our human family. I am not an indigenous person; my genes are a collective spiral of generations, but I feel very connected to the people speaking here because I, like everyone else, have ancient roots. Every one of us has tribal ancestors. Within us, we carry an ancient identity. The "spirit of indigenous peoples" resides in us, an eternal reminder of our deep-down connections.

Our tribal ancestors lived in deep connection with the natural world. They were at home on earth and with themselves. They developed a strong sense of security through knowing that they "belonged," that they were an integral part of the continuum of life. The essence of their being was rooted deep in their tribal territory, which was only vaguely distinguished from their cosmic territory. Primal, unspoiled, authentic, they lived their lives, daily, blending the animate with the inanimate, the temporal with the spiritual, and the personal with the communal. Indigenous to one area, they were universal thinkers.

From foragers and gatherers, a span of roughly fifty thousand years ago to ten thousand years ago, we all derive our common heritage. Many of us went on to be technological people: logical, analytical, exclusive, specialized, centralized. Others, small in number but large in spirit, have remained on the path of their ancestors: holistic, intuitive, inclusive, diversified, generalized. When we call these people "primitive," it means only that their way of life as a whole is organized along simpler lines, simpler living.

The challenge for most of us enveloped in a world of technology and materialism is to stay on our paths and still honor our original cultural pattern, our original nature. Kofi Annan, the Secretary-General of the United Nations, born in Ghana, Africa, wrote about the relationship between technology and humanity in an article entitled, "What Can I Do to Make Things Better?" "With only a click on a mouse," he wrote, "people from different continents can talk to each other. An e-mail message can get from me to you in seconds, whether you live in the United States, Japan, Africa, or South America. . . . Computers and modems help us talk and listen to each other across the world. But that wouldn't do us much good if we didn't already have a lot in common. And we do. We may have different religions, different languages, different colored skins, but we all belong to one human race. We all share the same basic values."

It can be daunting, confusing, as we sort our way through the many layers of life, folded one upon the other as civilization becomes more complex and intricate. Gustave Walter, a French anthropologist, said, "Where we see confusion, primitive man sees fusion."

Most of us are truly trying to make life simple. We are striving to create a workable pattern for our lives, a successful way to be human, a way that integrates all parts of our being: work, play, love, ritual, and reverence. The confusion and consternation sets in when we fail to see that one facet of our lives is nestled into another, and that into the next, and so on, creating our whole system of being, completely interactive and inclusive.

The Afar people of Ethiopia saw this. They fused all things into one being when they named a common ancestor of ours. We know this ancestor as Lucy. The Afar know her by the name of Dinquinesh. Lucy, a more-than-three-million-year-old hominid relative, was discovered in 1974 in the Afar Desert of northeastern Ethiopia. The anthropologists on the site named this tiny ancestor, not more than three and a half feet tall, after the Beatles tune, "Lucy in the Sky with Diamonds," the song that had accompanied them as they dug. But the Afar people chose the name "Dinquinesh," which means "Thou Art Wonderful." These nomadic people brought together the tribal and the cosmic — our wonderful human quality with our sacred, divine nature — all in one find. They went to the heart of our matter, honoring the foundations of human existence. Originally, traditionally, we are whole of heart.

With its more than 240 ethnic groups represented, *Simply Living* seeks to highlight the unity of all beings through our ancient identity. This wisdom collection speaks to us about what is native in all of us — the timeless truths, the universal principles, that bridge all time and place — or as Secretary-General Annan said, "the same basic values" we all share.

To be aware of patterns of culture throughout the world, those rooted deep in indigenous living, is to be aware of the enduring patterns in ourselves that foster respect, consideration, understanding, compassion, and wisdom. To be in tune with these parts of ourselves is to be filled with celebration for a world enriched and enlivened by cultural diversity.

It is my hope that this book of global wisdom joins in this celebration, where what is sacred to human nature is not taken for granted but honored and activated, preserved and nourished, in all its vibrant patterns.

Technological development can create a feeling of artificial scarcity, a conditioned response of never having enough money or goods. It is time to take a global journey that leads us to a deeper appreciation of our humanity and of the earth we inhabit. The Irish poet Seamus Heaney said it well when he made the plea to "economic man" to "return to more instinctual, spiritual, and mythically sanctioned habits of being."

There is always enough in being ourselves, whole-heartedly. "Enough is plenty," for the Balearic-Island villager who said these words, and for everyone.

— SHIRLEY ANN JONES

EDITOR'S NOTE

Simply Living explores perennial human themes that thread in and out of our lives and weave our pattern of existence.

We gain great insight by listening to people closely connected to basic existence, those ways passed down through generations of living that hold true to original truths. As life becomes more complex, we seek to find harmony and underlying order in our sometimes confusing maze of experiences. The quotations in this book stir our sense of inner knowingness. These global voices help us become more powerful interpreters of life, more indigenous to our true state, and more peaceful in our quest to understand the intricacies of life. We awaken to an intensively conscious awareness that pulses with full appreciation for who we are and where we are going, united in our individuality.

Simply Living can be read from front to back or back to front, finding a world of wisdom gathered together not as an aggregate but as an intricate of infused meaning. To shine light upon a life circumstance for a particular moment or day, you, the reader, can select an archetype (the seer, the seeker, the heartweaver...) or can choose a quote at random to discover how the passage connects, not always linearly, to your life.

Whether obtained through deliberate or random selection, the message here is clear: Life is a matter of simply living. The underlying order, the balance of being that indigenous cultures embrace exists for each of us, each and every day.

Simply Living

THE HERALDER
of CONSCIOUSNESS

HELLO: YOU'RE HERE

Qanoq sila? — "How is the universe?"

— NETSILIK ESKIMO GREETING
Northern Canada

Aga poi — "Good morning to you all."

— DOGON GREETING
Bandiagara cliffs, Mali, Africa

Está en su casa — "You are in your house."

— PERUVIAN GREETING TO GUESTS

Mi casa es su casa — "My house is your house."

— MEXCALTITÁN GREETING TO GUESTS
Island village of Mexcaltitán

Everywhere I went...I heard the Ponapean word of greeting. Interchangeable for either hello or goodbye, it is one of the world's loveliest words: *Kasalehlia!* When you hear it pronounced liltingly on the tongue — cassa-LAY-leeah — by a Ponapean maiden with a flower in her flowing hair, as you pass her thatched house under the palm trees beside the deep sea, you feel you have heard the sound of paradise.

— DAVID S. BOYER
"Micronesia: The Americanization of Eden"
Ponape District, Trust Territory of the Pacific Islands

In class I made points explaining that in Mexico roosters said "qui-qui-ri-qui" and not "cock-a-doodle-doo" to bring in the day, but after school I had to put up with the taunts of a big Yugoslav who said Mexican roosters were crazy.

— ERNESTO GALARZA
Born in the mountain village of Jalcocotán, western Mexico

I've been getting up earlier these days because of that old rooster we have. The older it gets, the earlier in the morning it goes "ku-kaREE-kwaa."

— VISHNU MAYA
Gurung tribe, central Nepal

U phela Joang? — "Are you well?"

— GREETING
People of Kingdom of Lesotho, Africa

Bula! — "What's happening?"

— GREETING
Republic of Fiji

We have no good morning or good night in our language. To a Burmese, a smile is more eloquent than words. Sometimes foreigners misunderstand. During World War II, a handbook printed for your GIs warned them not to read too much into a Burmese girl's smile;

she might just be saying hello — or good bye!

— U SAN WIN
Burmese native, Myanmar (formerly Burma)

As we beached on the rough, pebbled shore of Wagu village, people rushed toward us hugging, clinging, laughing, and crying. With each pair of eyes I met flowed thousands of silent thoughts. There is no Bahinemo word for "hello," and only an extended absence requires a greeting: "You're here."

— EDIE BAKKER
"Return to Hunstein Forest"
Papua New Guinea

T'an Bahktale! — "Good Fortune to You!"

— ROMA (GYPSY) GREETING
Russia

Staray ma-shi — "May you not be tired."

— PUSHTUN TRIBESMAN GREETING
Afghanistan

Namaste — "I salute the god within you."

— GREETING IN INDIA, NEPAL

Hau. Mitakuipi ampetu kile chante ma waste napa chuzau. — Greetings my relatives. Today is a good day, my heart is strong, and I extend my hand in friendship.

— WILLIAM MEANS
Lakota, South Dakota
President of the International Indian Treaty Council

HERE WE ARE

We the peoples of the United Nations determined...to reaffirm faith in fundamental human rights, in the dignity and worth of the human person...to practice tolerance and live together in peace with one another as good neighbors...have resolved to combine our efforts to accomplish these aims.

— CHARTER OF THE UNITED NATIONS, DRAFTED IN 1945

The Latin appellation for the sacredness of a place is "koltus" — culture.

— GEORGE J. DEMKO
Why in the World

The vision of the present is the vision of a single world living in peace and harmony, not under unified rule of a single power or through the adoption of a single cultural system, but rather through learning mutual respect for the different ways of peoples in other parts of the world. We need, each of us, to cherish our own culture for ourselves, while still recognizing that other peoples may find other ways of life more satisfying.

— WALTER GOLDSCHMIDT
Ways of Mankind

The movement of a culture of peace, like a great river, is fed from diverse streams — from every tradition, culture, language, religion, and political perspective. Its goal is a world in which this wealth of cultures lives together in an atmosphere marked by intercultural understanding, tolerance, and solidarity.

— FORUM ON THE CULTURE OF PEACE PROGRAMME
UNESCO

The essence of Frazer's achievements was that he saw the need to stand outside his own culture to understand other cultures.

— ABOUT SIR JAMES GEORGE FRAZER, AUTHOR
Foreword to *The Golden Bough*

Any acquaintance with anthropology is therefore bound to awaken a feeling of pride in the human race, the inexhaustible fertility of its power to create cultures. With that comes tolerance.

— GENE LISITZKY
Four Ways of Being Human

We need to share some values such as a commitment to fundamental human rights and basic rules of interaction, but we can be wildly different in other areas such as lifestyles, spirituality, musical tastes, and community life.

— JACK WEATHERFORD
Savages and Civilization — Who Will Survive?

As the traveler who has once been from home is wiser than he who has never left his own doorstep, so a knowledge of one other culture should sharpen our ability to scrutinize more steadily, to appreciate more lovingly, our own.

— MARGARET MEAD
Anthropologist

Each culture embodies an experiment in the human potential. Each culture stands as a monument to man's achievement, and each testifies to the human capacity to find a formula for survival. Yet each web may have so intricate and fragile a pattern that cutting the strands of religion, political life, or economic base can sometimes cause the whole delicate structure to collapse. The people stay on, but their special way of adapting to life may vanish.

— MATTHEW W. STIRLING
National Geographic Society

Foraging has been the most generalized and enduring subsistence pattern developed by humans. It is the only strategy proven viable over tens of thousands of years. All of us emerged only recently from this same foraging past, and none of us has quite adjusted to the sudden change in the human way of life. The aborigines, sitting ragged and dirty with the smell of alcohol on them, show the sudden transition and dislocation more clearly than we do, but our own "modern" society suffers from it just as much as theirs, if not more.

— JACK WEATHERFORD
Savages and Civilization — Who Will Survive?

The Native people have been here thousands and thousands of years, but take a look at the land and you cannot find a trace of where they've been. Western civilization has been here maybe 200 or 300 years, and you can see everywhere it's been.

— CLAUDE DEMIENTIEFF JR.
Yukon native, Alaska

The push to explore and exploit the remotest corners of the earth cannot be stopped easily, if at all.

— DAVID MAYBURY-LEWIS
Anthropologist

Ideas of superiority, delusions of grandeur and megalomania probably emerged with the first consciousness of man that his racial group was different from others. Wherever we meet the superiority theories, in antiquity or modern times, they are all extraordinarily alike. They constitute the faith of the unenlightened, maintained, of course, by the stupidity of the many and the cunning of the few.

— FRANZ BOAS
Anthropologist

The white man saves the whooping crane, he saves the goose in Hawaii, but he is not saving the way of life of the Indian.

— BLACKFOOT INDIAN
Expressed during the Alcatraz Island takeover

If, despite immense difficulties, we wean ourselves of this habit of regarding material achievements as culture, we shall have come a step nearer the most important truth of all: that the most advanced culture is not necessarily that with the fastest machines or the largest cities, and that there is no fundamental difference between the primitive and the civilized.

— CORNELIUS OSGOOD
Anthropologist, Ethnologist

We can no longer assume, if we are fortunate enough to live in one of the "developed" countries, that our way of life represents the most advanced stage of progress and that other societies have simply been less successful than ours in attaining it. Instead, we now know that other societies have made other choices, followed different paths in search of different destinies. This knowledge opens up new vistas on the richness and variety of what it means to be human. The challenge we all face is how to come to terms with these differences, how to live with the variety, now that we have discovered that there are more things in heaven and earth than were dreamt of in our philosophy.

— DAVID MAYBURY-LEWIS
Millennium: Tribal Wisdom and the Modern World

I was thinking of anthropology as the perfect educational tool it is — a mind stretcher, prejudice dissolver, and taste widener.

— GENE LISITZKY
Four Ways of Being Human

The ultimate value of anthropology is that it enables us to follow the dictum "Know thyself."

— WALTER GOLDSCHMIDT
Ways of Mankind

One never seduced by a foreign culture can never appreciate the fetters of his own. Life, after all, is a journey — a voyage of discovery. Why not take the high road?

— THOMAS J. ABERCROMBIE
"Prince of Travelers"

THE STORYTELLER
of OLD

ONCE UPON A CREATION

The beginning began with a sound. A sound that was music within the silence. It was dull but sweet, a golden sound that rang and echoed through the nothingness. It was constant and went ringing over, under, sideways, and through itself. It was the beginning, a start, a creation.

— JOHN ACTIVE
Yup'ik, born in Chukfaktoolik
A small western Eskimo village, Alaska

In the beginning, there was blackness. Only the sea. In the beginning there was no sun, no moon, no people. In the beginning there were no animals, plants. Only the sea. The sea was the Mother. The Mother was not people, she was not anything. Nothing at all. She was when she was, darkly. She was memory and potential. She was aluna.... Aluna is where the Law of the Mother began; it is the place of the spirit, of the mind, of intelligence. It is the place of thinking.

— THE KOGI HISTORY OF CREATION
Sierra Nevada, Colombia

From the conception, the increase; from the increase, the swelling; from the swelling, the thought; from the thought, the remembrance; from the remembrance, the consciousness, the desire.

— MAORI CREATION CHANT
New Zealand

In the very beginning of the Goajira genesis, therefore, there was Woman. She lived in solitude until, during one of her menstrual periods, she encountered a powerful thunderstorm and became pregnant. Her Boy Child is Maleíwa, the creator. Thus Maleiwa was born out of the eternal Woman without the agency of a man. The name of this "Urmutter" is Mother of Maleíwa.

— JOHANNES WILBERT
Survivors of Eldorado
On the legend of the Goajiro Indians
Colombia and Venezuela, South America

The two Djanggau Sisters came across the water traveling on the path of the rising sun from an island away to the northeast. They made the first people. They made the water holes and the sacred ritual sites. At first the sisters possessed all the most secret sacred objects, the most sacred rites. Men had nothing. And so men stole them. But the sisters said, "Oh, let them keep those things. Now men can do this work, looking after those things for everybody."

— AUSTRALIAN ABORIGINAL MYTH

In the beginning, there was no man. Flying through the darkness, the son of the bat fell in love with the daughter of the jatobá tree. Out of their love, two boys were born: the sun and the moon. The brothers made many bows and arrows and set them up next to each other in a long row. Then they made large cigars and blew the smoke against the bows and arrows, changing them into human beings —

the ancestors of the Indians who dwelt among the headwaters of the Xingu River.

— WAURÁ INDIANS
Creation Myth
Upper Xingu Region, Brazil

Our Father, the Sun, seeing that men lived like wild animals, took pity on them, and sent to earth a son and daughter of his, in order that they might teach men the knowledge of our Father the Sun, and that they might know how to cultivate plants and grains and make use of the fruits of the earth like men and not beasts. With these orders and mandate our Father the Sun placed his son and daughter in Lake Titicaca.

— LEGEND OF THE HIGH ANDEAN PLATEAU
Titicaca, Bolivia

Very, very when, all mankind lived underground at the bottom of a seven-storied subterranean mountain.

— HOPI LEGEND

A long time ago there was only one man living in all the forest. His name was Ochiosa, and one day God sent a woman to him so that he would not be lonely. Ochiosa had never seen a woman before and so thought that she had been wounded in the place where he expected a man's penis to be. Making some medicine from a vine of the forest, he put it in the wound and the woman later bore a son called Luembe, who was the first Mbuti.

— NDEKE
Ituri Forest, Democratic Republic of Congo, Africa

For his bones, I take the birches; for his flesh, the salmon and the stag; the black bear's hide shall be his hair, and the good red clay his skin. The dark of deep waters shall shine in the shadow of his eyes. His private spirit shall be strong magic and great medicine. His nature shall be noble, fiery, heaven-bent, and proud. And in the book of the world, his name shall be written: Man.

— IROQUOIS STORY OF CREATION

For her bones I take the slim white clouds; for her flesh, the dove and the doe; the blackbird's gloss shall glitter in her hair, and sweet fruit ripen in her skin. The black tears of the pine tree shall be melted in her eyes. Her private spirit shall be great medicine and strong magic. Her nature shall be yielding, unpredictable, resilient, and bright. And in the book of the world, her name shall be written: Woman.

— IROQUOIS STORY OF CREATION

In the beginning, God gave to every people a cup of clay, and from this cup they drank their life.

— DIGGER INDIAN LEGEND
California

My strength is from the fish; my blood is from the fish, from the roots and the berries. The fish and the game are the essence of my life. I was not brought from a foreign country and did not come here. I was put here by the Creator.

— MENINOCK
Yakima Indian

In Ketchikan they tell the story of a Haida lad who returned home from grade school greatly upset. "The teacher said it wasn't true that we were descended from the raven, like you said," the boy told his father. "Now sit down, son," the father said firmly. "I want to have a talk with you. You were descended from the raven. The white man may be descended from the monkey, but you were descended from the raven!"

> — LAEL MORGAN
> On the Haida of Southeastern Alaska

Many, many years ago, men lived under the ground, and all the world was a rock. They lived with their animals far below. Then one day a man and his wife were following a monkey that their dog was chasing through an endless rock tunnel. After a long trip they emerged on the surface of the world, a great black flat rock. They returned home, gathered seeds and worms, and brought them to the surface. Soon the seeds sprang up and the worms multiplied and life on the earth began.

> — Y BANG R LIK
> A Mnong village elder, Buon Rocai, Vietnam

Then the Creator and the Maker asked, "Can you not see? Can you not hear? Your language and your way of walking, are they not good? Look around you then! Contemplate the world! See if the mountains and valleys do not appear! Try then to see!" Thereupon the men saw all that there was in the world. The men thanked the Creator and the Maker. Verily, we thank ye, over and over...we are in possession of our senses, and we are acquainted with all that is far and near. We also see the large and the small in the heavens and on earth....But the Creator and the Maker were not pleased with what they had heard. "It is not right what our creatures, our handiwork, say; they know everything, the large and the small," they said. Then the Heart of the Sky cast a vapor over their eyes, which were clouded as when one blows upon a mirror. Their eyes were misted and they could see only what was near. Only that was clear to them. So were destroyed the wisdom and knowledge....

> — MAYAN LEGEND

The way of my teachings is that the creation came into being, all the trees, animals, insects; then at the end was mankind. We were supposed to be his most wonderful creation, and yet they always tell us that we have to be more humble than the insects, the lowest, crawling creature.

— BERTHA GROVE
Southern Ute Indian Reservation, Colorado

We think of ourselves as custodians of the land, and the land's not just soil and rock to us. It's the whole of creation — all the land, water, and air, and the life everywhere, people, too. All these things are related and linked together in the Dreamtime.

— PAULINE GORDON
Aboriginal, Bunjalung tribe, Australia

It's my understanding from our legends that the reason we have the four colors is that we were all children of God. Not four races, but one race of four different colors: white clay, red clay, black clay, and yellow clay. And we feel that all people were given original instructions from Creator. Those who have gotten away from them have suffered.

— MIKE HANEY
Lakota/Seminole

There's a story that the gods were talking one day, all gathered up, and they said, "Wait a minute now. Here we got man and he's got all this power. He's got all this potential. Man is a part of us . . . but he hasn't come to the point to where he knows what to do with this. What are we going to do?" They said, "We've got to hide it from him." One said, "Let's put it in the bottom of the ocean." Another said, "No, no, he'll go down there. . . . " "Let's put it up in the sky." "No, no, one day he's going to fly up there. . . . " "Well, let's bury it deep in the earth." "No. He'll dig. He'll dig it up." "Well, where are we going to put it?" One said, "Let's go to the big god, the wisest of all, and ask him." So they went to the wisest and they asked, "Where are we going to hide this from man?" He said, "Put it within him. He'll never look there."

> — LEANDIS
> A Mexican healer, northern Mexico

When you think how things are, and you don't know how they began and how they will go on, and you don't know whether they will end, then you can go on thinking and thinking — and never stop.

> — WEST AFRICAN SAYING

Every shape has its own power. Every form makes energy patterns. A circle bends the energies from its area inside and out, back onto itself, round and round, and creates a spiral.

> — CHEA HETAKA
> Brazilian Indian, western Amazon basin

You have noticed that everything an Indian does is in a circle, and that is because the Power of the World always works in circles, and everything tries to be round. . . . The Sky is round and I have heard that the earth is round like a ball and so are all the stars. The Wind, in its greatest power, whirls. Birds make their nests in circles, for theirs is the same religion as ours. The sun comes forth and goes down again in a circle. The moon does the same, and both are round. Even the seasons form a great circle in their changing, and always come back again to where they were. The life of a man is a circle from childhood to childhood, and so it is in everything where power moves.

> — HEHAKA SAPA
> Oglala Sioux

As a human race, we have moments of incredible greatness, not power and control over things, but power to connect with Po-wa-ha, "water-wind-breath," the creative energy of the world, the breath that makes the wind blow and the waters flow.

— RINA SWENTZELL
Santa Clara Pueblo Indian

I wish to give you a message from "Omama." "Omama" is the creator of the Yanomami and the creator of the "shaboris," who are our shamans. The "shaboris" have all the knowledge, and they have sent us to deliver their message.... Our word is to protect nature, the wind, the mountains, the forest, the animals, and this is what we want to teach you.

— DAVID YANOMAMAI
Yanomami Tribe, Amazon, Brazil

THE PLANTER
of ROOTS

ANCIENT MOORINGS

Hoy, y siempre — "Yesterday, today, and always."

— ECUADORIAN SAYING

Of all human existence, 99 percent was life in primitive society, as a fraction remains today. If for no other reason than this, we should be curious about it.

— ELMAN R. SERVICE
"The Ghosts of Our Ancestors"

I have never been psychoanalyzed. The close study of primitive people is another way of arriving at insight.

— MARGARET MEAD
Anthropologist
Some Personal Views

The so-called primitive peoples are closer in their culture to the beginnings of the human race. They are aware of the origins of their existence and still mindful of the ladder that leads to God.

— IVAR LISSNER
Ethnologist

What is the meaning of primitive experience? I have tried many times to sum it up, at least for myself....It means, I think, man confronted by raw nature and answering the challenge with all the incalculable resources of his physical skill, wits, and imagination. The result is anything you want to call it — good or bad — but it surely amounts to the widest range of behavior that any living thing on this planet is capable of. There is no single primitive way.

— LEWIS COTLOW
In Search of the Primitive

Who are the Inadan? Legend describes them as "older than memory, proud as the crow, mischievous as the wind."

— MICHAEL AND AUBINE KIRTLEY
"The Inadan: Artisans of the Sahara"
Describing the blacksmiths in the Tuareg society in Niger, Africa

Anywhere on this earth I walk I would have to go through four layers of earth to get through this crust to get to the middle of the earth. That's how long we have been here, how long our people have lived and died here. When I walk here, I walk on the bones of my ancestors.

— MIKE HANEY
Lakota/Seminole

Before God was God and boulders were boulders, the Basques were already Basques.

— OLD BASQUE SAYING

They say we have been here for 60,000 years, but it is much longer. We have been here since the time before time began. We have come directly out of the Dreamtime of the Creative Ancestors. We have lived and kept the earth as it was on the First Day.

— ABORIGINAL TRIBAL ELDER
Australia

As a Kenyan, I can trace my ancestry back two million years.

— IZIAH ODHIAMBO NENGO
Kenyan native

It becomes clearer with each passing year that this is precisely the greatest need of all Americans: a continental history. By this I mean a whole, fully integrated history of this continent from the granitic base of the land mass itself, up through the layers of soil to the grasses and plants, the trees, the huge geological configurations; the animals who lived and died out and those that still live; the first men who, following those animals, crossed the widening and narrowing land strait; the rise of cultures here and their myths which describe for us how it felt to stand defenseless in a gigantic landscape. . . . An enormous undertaking, this five billion year history, but one that must be seriously begun if we are to understand who we are and where we ought to be headed.

— FREDERICK W. TURNER III
Introduction, *I Have Spoken*

Maybe we ought to look back to primitive peoples to find out where the world went wrong. There seems to be a growing sense that it has gone wrong. Maybe we can learn from the Tasadays.

— KENNETH MACLEISH
"The Tasadays: Stone Age Cavemen of Mindanao"
On a tribe living in the Philippines

Despite the etymology of "civilization" from "city" and the development of the word "savage" from the Latin word for "forest," the most savage way of life is now found in the centers of our most modern cities. Civilization has produced a savagery far worse than that which we once imputed to primitive tribes.

— JACK WEATHERFORD
Savages and Civilization — Who Will Survive?

I knew that the village people, in times of crisis, believe that they have been cursed either by some evil spirit or by a witch or sorcerer, but not the Pygmies. Their logic is simpler and their faith stronger because their world is kinder.

> — COLIN M. TURNBULL
> *The Forest People: A Study of the Pygmies of the Congo*

Nothing is more gentle than man in his primitive state.

> — JEAN JACQUES ROUSSEAU
> French philosopher

Not all, but most primitive peoples are free of the terrible self-righteousness that makes the person who is "free of sin" — either in appearance or by dint of an extraordinary denial of his impulses — feel that he has the right, sometimes even the duty, to inflict cruelty on a hapless victim, too often a small and helpless child.

> — MARGARET MEAD
> *Some Personal Views*

No one who has carried out research among the oldest primitive peoples can fail to understand that they possess a lively awareness of a supreme being and are deeply convinced of his omnipotence and goodness.

> — IVAR LISSNER
> Ethnologist

I can't think of any word less appropriate than primitive. I find people in the rural area conscious of what affects them. They are very intelligent people.

> — DONALD F. HEISEL
> Research sociologist
> On the Masai, the Turkana, and the Somalis, Eastern Africa

The so-called primitive peoples possess a spiritual culture and a delicacy of thought and feeling which we have always underestimated.

— IVAR LISSNER
Ethnologist

If in our lifetime we suppress nomads, we shall have done by human harshness what natural harshness could not do. To abolish nomads because they have other skills, know other things, hold other aspirations, and live by other customs than ours — in short, because they are different — is as unwise as it is unworthy.

— NEVILLE DYSON-HUDSON
"Nomadic Peoples Find Freedom and Identity in the Life They Follow"

We must learn to do something which Europeans find immensely difficult: to unlearn the habit of constantly applying our own standards to the cultures of primitive peoples.

— IVAR LISSNER
Ethnologist

In no event can the Stone Age Indian ever be the same again, and that is why each "sertanista," or Indian expert, carries in his heart "saudade," a nostalgic sadness. For he must live with the knowledge that whether he brings stark tragedy or better lives to the people of the forest, he will unavoidably diminish a simple, fragile beauty the world can never see again.

— W. JESCO VON PUTTKAMER
"Brazil Protects Her Cinta Largas"
On the Cinta Largas Indian of Brazil

The value of primitive societies is that they provide a "mirror for man."

— WALTER GOLDSCHMIDT
Ways of Mankind

HERITAGE TO HOLD

To get the confidence we need to improve our lives, we have to develop pride in ourselves by discovering who we are and who we were.

— JOHN JOE SARK
Micmac, Prince Edward Island, Canada

You really never know who a man is until you know who his grandfather and his ancestors are.

— PUNJABI VILLAGER
Punjab province of Pakistan

I think I'd ask other peoples of the world to respect their ancestors. When you know your ancestors, you respect yourself.

— AMARU
Quechuan Indian, Peru

Many people in the West have been uprooted from their traditions, their cultural roots. And this is my fear for my people. If we are pulled up from our roots, what happens? If you uproot a tree or a flower, it will die. I think a lot of people in the West have been uprooted and have become spiritual drifters.

— MUTANG URUD
Kelabit tribesman
Borneo, Malay Peninsula

You see, it happens sometimes that when a people of ancient culture come into the modern world, they are in such a hurry to catch up they throw away all that reminds them of the past. I, too, felt like this when I was a girl...but one day it happened that a Russian girl from Leningrad, who had become my close friend, asked me to make her a pair of our embroidered boots and a reindeer fur jacket. She said her people had nothing so beautiful. Afterward I began to think perhaps we were being too hasty. Over the years I came to realize we must remain Yakut; to turn ourselves into Russians would be to lose ourselves, as some stranger might lose himself in the depths of the taiga.

— ELENE EREMEVINA AMOSOVA
Yakut Eskimo, Siberia

She always said good Indians remember two things: their humor and their history. These are the elements that dictate our culture and our survival in this crazy world. If these are somehow destroyed or forgotten, we would be doomed to extinction. Our power gone.

— ROGER JACK
Indian, Pacific Northwest
Reminiscing about his Aunt Greta

If you forget who you are, you cannot live in peace. That's why I enjoy showing people that my culture is alive and well.

— OMAR SUAZO
Garifuna, Central America

We are Bedouin. It is our life.

— JABR
Bedouin-Murrah tribesman, Saudi Arabia

It is the custom *this* way.

— MANUEL CRESPO
Villager, highlands of Guatemala

We wish to live in peace in our mountains, according to our customs.

— SENTIMENT OF THE MURUNGS
Chittagong Hill Tracts, Bangladesh

We say only three things are sacred to a gaucho. His horse, which is his freedom from the earth. His facón [knife], which is his companion and protector in a fight. And his "china," his woman.

— MEZA
A Gaucho, South American grasslands, Argentina

Every Indian has the blood of the tribal memory circling his heart. . . . Today more and more Indians are coming back, not to the despair that has marked reservation life but to the strong sound of the drum.

— SHERMAN ALEXIE
Coeur d'Alene Indian, Washington

We've got it made. We can still go out and hunt and gather. I'm rich in a different sense. I still have a culture, an opportunity to do whatever I want. The spirit is still in me.

— DIXIE DAYO
Eskimo from Manley Hot Springs, a village near Fairbanks, Alaska

We live for our ceremonies. Through them we maintain contact with our ancestors who made the land before us. We have ceremonies to make men and ceremonies for death.

— NANDJIWARRA AMAGULA
Aboriginal, Arnhem Land
Northeast frontier of Australia's Northern Territory

When myths fade from a people's memory, when their traditions lose importance, when old values no longer serve a need — the world loses something unique and precious.

— MATTHEW W. STIRLING
Committee for Research and Exploration
National Geographic Society

I used to know several Indian languages, but I think I've swallowed them with my rice.

— VISHNU MAYA
Gurung tribe, central Nepal

The roots are still alive, but it's painful not to see young people pick up on the culture. They go to high school and learn to like white sugar....

— JOSH WEISER
Yup'ik, Bethel, Alaska

I wish more people would share the ways of their grandmothers. I think it would help the present world situation if we all learned to value and respect the ways of the grandmothers — our own as well as everyone else's.

— BEVERLY HUNGRY WOLF
Blood Indian Reserve, Canada

Have respect to me, a setting sun, a fallen tree, stricken by many waters.

— MAORI PROVERB
New Zealand, on respect of the elderly

Stop pruning my leaves and taking away my hoe. Enough of drowning my beliefs and chopping up my roots. Have done with suffocating my mind. No more of killing my chants and silencing my voice. …Grandparents' gifts are not dimmed, rich memory, ancestral blood: rituals of remembrance.…Give us light, faith, and life in the sacred rites.

— ELIANE POTIGUARA
Brazilian Indian

The more I think about myself, the more I feel like a little boat in the ocean or like a sand in the desert. Why God didn't make me as a cloud or make me as a wind so I could fly in the pretty blue sky. I wish I go back to my dear beautiful country, but the distance is so far to me, and I think I lose my country.

— MAU
Cambodian teenager

My country, take care of your light!

— PABLO NERUDA
Chilean, Chile

We vow to control again our own destiny and recover our complete humanity and pride in being Indigenous People.

— FINAL STATEMENT
First International Conference of Indigenous Peoples
Port Alberni, British Columbia, 1975

I do not know if you are receiving my letters, but I will keep writing to you as you are always in my mind.... We have made an altar to Father. We try to keep up our traditions so that we can look forward to the day we can return to our country, although we do not know when that will be. Here we are materially well off, but spiritually deprived. We miss our country. Most of all we miss you. Should Buddha exist, we should keep praying to be reunited. Dear Mother, keep up your mind. Pray to Buddha silently. We will have a future, and I hope it will be soon.

— TRAN THI NGA
Living in Connecticut, writing to her mother in Vietnam

In my heart, I cannot ignore the old greatness. A people with no past is nothing.

— POLYNESIAN VILLAGER
Rarotonga, Cook Islands

It is very difficult to learn everything about a people — the language, customs, and culture — just by reading written reports. What makes all those things meaningful to us of Aleut descent is the "remembering." Remembering stories of the past that we heard in childhood from the elderly of our villages. Remembering the clothing, boats, skis, traps, toys, weapons, tools, and baskets that we have seen or used and know are authentic remnants of the past.... Remembering how the soft, beautiful language was spoken; how it sounded in a roomful of people with everyone talking at once; how it sounded in the open when a hunting trip was concluding and the village people were gathering to receive their shares of the bounty. Remembering the smell of various concoctions used by our people for medicine.... Even though this remembering by one individual may seem insignificant, it is important because it adds to the complete picture of the Aleut heritage.

— LILLIE MCGARVEY
Born and reared in the Aleutian Islands
in the village of Unalaska, Alaska

These isolated hill people declare they once had scriptures written on banana leaves, but a cow ate them. Since that day, a cow has paid the penalty each year at harvest time.

— BERN KEATING
A journalist on the Murung tribesmen
Chittangong Hill Tract, Bangladesh

My father saved all of our family's extra money to buy a tape recorder. This was such an expensive thing for him to buy, I didn't understand then the importance of what he was doing. You see, with no written language, our people were superb storytellers. The stories contained all the wisdom of our people. My father has now recorded more than five hundred hours of Ainu stories that would have been lost.

— SHIRO KAYANO
Ainu tribe
Island of Hokkaido, Japan

I love to talk to the old Basques. There are so few left. We owe them so much for what they went through in those hills to give us, their children, our start in this country. If we turn out half the men they were, it will be enough.

— JOE DE ARRIETA
Basque, Pyrenees border region of France and Spain

To know my history, I had to put away my books and return to the land. I had to plant taro in the earth before I could understand the inseparable bond between people and "aina" [land]. I had to feel again the spirits of nature and take gifts of plants and fish to the ancient alters. I had to begin to speak my language with our elders and leave long silences for wisdom to grow. But before anything else, I had to learn the language like a lover so that I could rock within her and lay at night in her dreaming arms.

— HAUNANI-KAY TRASK (HAUNANIOKAWEKIU)
Native woman of Hawaii

Once I spent five days alone, snowed in on Mont Blanc in the French Alps. I decided that if I survived I'd search our past for what makes us tick and build an honest Slovak house.

— PAVOL REPKA
Slovak, Slovak Socialist Republic

If you are born under a ceiling beam with a carved rosette, spanked with your nose buried in the embroidered front of your father's trousers, and have your tears dried on your mother's flowery skirt — you can never escape. These things will show in your work 30 years later.

— MIECZYSLAW BIERNACIK
Zakopane artisan, Poland

A person once asked me what my culture and lifestyle was. I told them it's something you have to live with to understand. It is something you cannot buy in the store, trade, or give away; it is something that you are born into.

— KENNETH JOHNS
Ahtna Indian, Alaska, Copper River

When I returned to Atka after World War II, my buddies asked me, "Why are you going back to the Aleutians? They say even the sea gulls are leaving there." I told him I was going because it's peaceful and quiet.

— DAN PROKOPEUFF

Aleut, Alaska

When I feel I have to force my smile, I know it's time to come home.

— MEXICAN WOMAN

Whose work takes her away from her fishing village in

Guanajuato, Mexico

Many people have said that indigenous peoples are myths of the past, ruins that have died. But the indigenous community . . . is full of vitality and has a course and a future. It has much wisdom and richness to contribute.

— RIGOBERTA MENCHU

Quiche native, Guatemala

This harpoon head is estimated to be over 2,000 years old. It was found on St. Lawrence Island. This is our proof to base our beliefs with. As you can see, it is much older than the Alaska Constitution and the U. S. Constitution. Our forefather's "file cabinet" was the permafrost. This is our proof that through subsistence our people have managed to survive for centuries. So much is at stake. We are not about to give up our inherent right to pass our baton of identity to the next generation. Not after over 2,000 years of doing so. Our forefathers are cheering and rooting for us in the stands.

— MERLE APASSINGOK

Savoonga, St. Lawrence Island, Alaska

I believe that culture belongs to the whole world. To keep our Ainu culture isn't just for us or the Japanese — it enriches the world.

— SHIRO KAYANO

Ainu tribe, The island of Hokkaido, Japan

I am "nan stlaay tuwaa kwiiuwaas" [precious greasy hands]. I am the mother of two Haida children, and I am proud to be here with you now. When I hear different speakers say, tonight, the Haida people have only their culture and their heritage, I want to say that the Haida people have their children. I am proud to be part of this Haida family that comes together now to celebrate all of their children. We are here to remember the strength and the sharing of our family, and we do it for ourselves and for our children. Thank you!

— SUSAN DAVIDSON
Haida Nation, Alaska
Speaking at a potlatch, a ceremony of sharing and giving

STURDY SEEDLINGS

We count the nine months a child spends in its mother's womb, and everyone considers himself a year older.

— RINZIN DORJI
Bhutanese villager, Bhutan

We are planted here. Man is a plant that grows and branches and flowers on earth.

— NAHUATL-SPEAKING DESCENDANT OF THE AZTECS, MEXICO
Upon burying the placenta of his child

We are each planted here to learn and express in our own individual ways, different aspects of the Great Spirit that is all things.

— COURTNEY DAVIS
Native Celt, South Wales

A Balinese, like a tree, must remember that he is strung between two worlds, balanced between the pull of gravity and the pull of heaven. Both the very young and the very old are seen as being particularly close to the Upper World. A Balinese child does not touch the ground for the first three months of life. He is cradled and cosseted above the earth and introduced to gravity very gently. When he is 105 days old a "foot-touching-the-ground" ceremony is held, when the child is ritually "planted" in matter, and first sets foot on the earth. Until then he has merely been an angel, hovering at the frontiers of the heavenly world. He is even weighed down with bracelets and anklets, to discourage him from floating up again too soon.

— LAWRENCE BLAIR
Ring of Fire

As soon as a child was old enough to walk, its parents took it into the woods and fields and taught it about the kamui [spirit] in nature. Soon that child had faith. As he grew older and developed his ability to comprehend, his faith was enhanced.... In those days we prayed for our children on many occasions. Maybe we have neglected to do so and should again pray for them.

— MISAO KAIZAWA
Ainu woman dancer, Hokkaido, Japan

The Pawnee child was born into a community from the beginning, and he never acquired the notion that he was closed in "within four walls." He was literally trained to feel that the world around him was his home — "kahuraru," the universe, meaning literally the inside land, and that his house was a small model of it. The infinite cosmos was his constant source of strength and his ultimate progenitor, and there was no reason why he should hesitate to set out alone and explore the wide world, even though years should pass before he returned. Not only was he not confined within four walls, but he was not closed in with a permanent group of people. The special concern of his mother did not mean that he was so closely embedded with her emotionally that he was not able to move about.

— GENE WELTFISH
"The Pawnee Person," in *The Lost Universe*

When I was a child, I had to stay with my father near the fire, up to twelve o'clock by night. It is good that children go to school and learn things, but that is not all. They should be like boys in former days and listen to the stories of their fathers and see how their fathers make the drums and the baskets and the pots. If they are just going to read books, their culture will die.

— ANDREA ZUNGUMBIA ZANDE
Subsistence farmer, Sudan

You see, as a Cree man, you usually don't tell your son, "Go split some wood for me." You go out and do it yourself. You let your kids watch you. We call it shadowing, and this spring I'll be starting it with my five-year-old son. When I take him out trapping with me, I'm not going to tell him what to do, just let him observe so he can see what it's all about. In this way, he'll learn how to work and to love the land. As we take more trips together, the land will become a part of him.

— ROBBIE NIQUANICAPPO
Cree, Quebec

Toddlers have only dirt, balls of dung, and empty tin cans to play with, but as they grow, imagination and enterprise come into use. A pestle balanced across a mortar becomes a seesaw. Mats of woven plant stems become playhouses.

— CAROLE E. DEVILLERS
"Oursi, Magnet in the Desert," Songhai of Oursi
Upper Volta village, southern rim of the Sahara

My students brought their exposed film to school and developed it in the little darkroom I built in a room of a colonial house in the village. During all these months they never damaged a roll of film; few experienced photographers could say the same. Being careful came naturally to the children. They had been making pots since they were five years old.

— WENDY EWALD
Magic Eyes
On teaching in the village of Ráquira, Colombia

Older persons in our kotan [village settlement] often told us children to appreciate our natural resources, especially our trees and rivers. We were to be careful not to damage or destroy young trees when we played in the woods or to set fire to the trees. Trees, our old people said, hold water which comes forth from the earth when it is needed. Trees on mountains, too, are the homes of our bear and deer. We were taught to respect our rivers and not to pollute them. They were the home of our fish. As children we were taught that mutual help of any kind was a great virtue.

— RANKOSHIA
Ainu elder, Hokkaido, Japan

I was taught all the ceremonies of "respecto" — the proper greetings for delivering messages to the neighbors; to press myself against the walls to allow adults to pass me on the narrow sidewalks; to speak only when addressed and not to put my spoon into adult conversation; never to show that I was bored with the questions adults asked me when we were visiting; never under any circumstances to ask for anything to eat; to enter the house with my cap in my hand; to answer instantly when called; to address everyone as señor or señora; and to talk quietly in conversation. Breaches of these rules of "respecto" fell somewhere between a sin and a crime.

— ERNESTO GALARZA
Barrio Boy
Born in Jalcocotán, a mountain village in western Mexico

My seven aunts are Ravens [clan name]. They have strongly supported me over the years. Nonnie (grandmother) told them, "You've got to help this guy." She has been the main influence in the family. She brought me up, she pushed me to be thoughtful.

— ROBERT DAVIDSON
Haida Nation, Alaska

Our family is a second school for our children. Our parents pass on to us their life experience, and we help them in their old age.

— MARIJKA POTJAK
Hutsul, Carpathian Mountains, southern Ukraine

Our elders never became senile because they were needed right to the end. Aunts and uncles on the mother's side were the ones who taught you the philosophies and principles that you lived and worked by.... You are taught that leadership is not for prestige, it's not for power, it's not for control, it's strictly for responsibility. And we lived by the honor code because there was no written language. You had to honor one another's word.

— LAVINA WHITE
Haida Nation, Alaska

Mama brought me up not to go looking for bad thoughts, and if I had any, to pray.

— ALICIA VÁSQUEZ
Born in Pan de Azúcar, Colombian Andes, South America

In our tradition we have a code of behavior which emphasizes "sem-teende," reserve and modesty; "munyal," patience and fortitude; and "hakkilo," care and forethought. This code, along with our many taboos, was given to us by our ancestors.

— MOKAO
Wodaabe native, Niger, Africa

I thank my grandmothers for my strong sense of self-esteem and cultural identity. They taught me that everything happens to you for a reason and that you must always look for the lesson in whatever occurs. Looking back, I realize that these outstanding women were the ones responsible for giving me the strength to be who I am. Not only were they extremely generous, but they knew how to honor people in simple ways, thereby empowering one to realize their potential.

— CAROLE ANNE HEART LOOKING HORSE
Rosebud/Yankton Sioux from South Dakota

It is a part of what makes me a "genuine Yup'ik." I thank my grandmother who taught me these things, who taught me to appreciate our subsistence lifestyle, to not waste, but share; to not steal, but provide for myself; to remember my elders, those living and dead and share with them; to be watchful at all times that I do not offend the spirits of the fish and animals; to give the beaver or seal that I caught a drink of water so its spirit would not be thirsty; to take from the land only what I can use; and to give to the needy if I have enough to share.

— JOHN ACTIVE
Yup'ik Eskimo, Bethel, southwest Alaska

My grandmother expected me to learn Hawaiian values and traditions. She was teaching me "lokahi" — spirit, harmony, unity.

— PUA CASE LAPULAPU
Native Hawaiian, Big Island

When I was young, the teacher spanked me, the priest spanked me, my father spanked me. Three big men tried to make a good citizen out of one little boy. Today they don't spank in school, the priest is less visible, and parents are busy working.

— SLOVAK VILLAGER
Slovak Socialist Republic

When a young man kills much meat he comes to think of himself as a chief or a big man, and he thinks of the rest of us as his servants or inferiors. We can't accept this. We refuse one who boasts, for someday his pride will make him kill somebody. So we always speak of his meat as worthless. This way we cool his heart and make him gentle.

— TOMAZO
Kung! Bushman, Kalahari Desert, Africa

If you were past six and going on seven, life in Jalco could be made disagreeable by neighbors who seemed to think that they could scold you and tell you how to behave. You never knew when a "compadre" or "comadre" of your aunt, or your uncle, or your father, or your mother was watching. For that matter, even people who were not "compadres" to your family thought they had some sort of rights over you. If you did or said something slightly irregular at the farthest end of the street from your cottage, where your legitimate bosses lived, somebody would be watching and ready to call out: "Mira, que muchachito tan malcriado." And if the offense was considered serious, the voice would say, "You will see, I am going to tell your mother." In a village so full of snitchers and busybodies you could get an extra ear-pull for any trivial breach of good manners — the "buena educacion" which the adults prized so highly.

— ERNESTO GALARZA
Barrio Boy
Born in Jalcocotán, a mountain village in western Mexico

In the Yup'ik language, the same word means both listen and obey. When children listen to their parents, they obey them.

YUP'IK ESKIMO CUSTOM
West Coast of Alaska

A disobedient three- or four-year-old child is old enough to understand when he is told that bad birds will come to fetch him or that bandits will come from the mountains, snatch him, and run away with him. But no one should say to a child, "Ghosts or monsters will come to get you!" for they might actually do so.

— TARO SASAKI
Ainu man of Hokkaido, Japan

We have four children, and they have brought us another four, and now we have ten grandchildren. Of course, they didn't always walk the path that we would choose them to be on all of the time. Now I see that in allowing them freedom to go out and experience whatever life holds for them is where our only responsibility lies. We have to be understanding enough to allow them to do that because we never know what experience they need in order to perfect themselves.

— SARA SMITH
Mohawk Tribe, Iroquois Confederacy

If the child is punished too often, or too severely, he will become perverse and ill-natured. He will no longer listen to anyone; he will develop a warped mind. The punishment should be such that the child realizes he has done wrong. The correction over with, the child should be shown affection. We call this "chopchopse-kara" in Ainu; it is an old custom; it gives the child the security he needs....If a child is singled out and corrected, he will become worse. If he feels that he is an odd one in the family, he will become more odd. A child must be corrected, but he must be given affection and security, as I already told you. It is like this: I scold and correct Kazuma... when he is not conforming, but as soon as he obeys, I call him to myself and give him a kiss. This is an old Ainu way.

— TARO SASAKI
Ainu tribe, Hokkaido, Japan

If a child does not know who they are by the time they are four years old, they might have to spend a lifetime discovering who they are. Their parents are supposed to protect them so they can develop in the right way. We believe that a child is born innocent. When they're four, they take on their own karma. Up until then, their parents are responsible.

— VERNON HARPER
Northern Cree, Canada

You bring a child into the world, you nurture it, you cultivate it, and you honor what they choose to become. You leave it at that. Then it's their job, again, to do that, to have children and nurture them and honor who they become.

— GEORGIA EPALOOSE
Zuni, New Mexico

I would like to make a difference.

— SCHOOLCHILD
Alwar, India

The pain you will feel is symbolic. There is a deeper meaning in all this. Circumcision means a break between childhood and adulthood. For the first time in your life, you are regarded as a grownup.... You will be expected to give and not just to receive. To protect the family always, not just to be protected yourself. And your wise judgment will for the first time be taken into consideration. No family affairs will be discussed without your being consulted. If you are ready for all these responsibilities, tell us now. Coming into manhood is not simply a matter of growth and maturity.... I have spoken.

— FATHER'S WORDS TO TEPILIT OLE SAITOTI
Before a Masai warrior initiation
Kenya, Africa

We call it Sunrise Dance. But it lasts through four days. It's the biggest ceremony of the White Mountain Apache — when a girl passes from childhood to womanhood. When my time came at 14, I didn't want to have one. I felt embarrassed. But my parents really wanted it.... I'm really glad I had a Sunrise Dance. It made me realize how much my parents care for me and want me to grow up right. They know my small age is past and treat me like a woman. If I have a daughter, I want her to have a Sunrise Dance too.

— NITA QUINTERO
Apache, Fort Apache Reservation, Arizona

We love our daughters and sons the same. We bear the burden of both for nine months, and there is no difference in the birth pangs. Sadly, our daughters must leave us to become part of another family. But then, our sons bring home someone else's daughters to carry on our lineage....

— KEOTIWALI
Villager in Nimkhera, India

I believe in dreams but not being a dreamer myself I only know what every child learns from his mother, for mothers tell children stories at bedtime to put them to sleep and it is from these stories we learn about things. I have never forgotten the old tales I heard from my mother. I have told them to my children and grandchildren, and I will tell them to you.

— NETSILIK OF CANADA

Grandmother says daylight is wiser than the dark. Let us sleep now and plan tomorrow.

— ISHI, LAST OF THE YAHI TRIBE
Western foothills of Mount Lassen, California

THE SEEKER
of WHOLENESS

WHO AM I?

Who are you? What are you? Where do you come from? Is it from the sun or the moon?

— POLAR ESKIMO

If you don't know who you are, you cannot know where you are going.

— SENDY VAUGHN SUAZO
Garifuna, Central America

Since everything is ultimately made out of the same atoms, there's no reason why we can't put them together to create whatever we want.

— TSERING DORJE
Ladakhi, N.E. Kashmir, Indian-Tibet border

Man has been possessed by a creative urge since very ancient times. Forever impelled to experiment and explore, it is as if he senses something within him which he must extract and examine so that, seeing it, he will know something of his own personality.

— IVAR LISSNER
Ethnologist

It takes years to learn to be the type of person you have to be. It's not like going to school where you graduate from four years of college and then you know everything.

— BERTHA GROVE
Southern Ute Indian Reservation, Colorado

Few of us can measure up to Immanuel Kant, who never left East Prussia yet felt he was a "Weltburger," a citizen of the world, not of a particular nation. In a profoundly examined life Kant posed three eternal questions: "What can I know? What ought I to do? What may I hope?"

— PRIIT J. VESILIND
National Geographic Senior Writer

Curiously enough, tribal peoples seem to have much less problem maintaining their own identity than we do. It is we who are constantly worried by our identity and feel it is threatened by diversity, multiculturalism, and so on.

— DAVID MAYBURY-LEWIS
Millennium: Tribal Wisdom and the Modern World

Establishing self-pride among the young is one of the most important goals. It's hard to be productive if you don't have pride in what you are.

— CLIFF ALLEN
Nez Perce Indian, Idaho

The family is very important to us here. It gives us security. You are not facing the world alone; you are also responsible for other people. Knowing the honor of the family is involved, you are a lot more careful of what you do.

— KIM KWANG SIK
Korean villager, South Korea

Some of our children become strangers to their own people. But much worse, they are strangers to themselves.

— YUP'IK MOTHER
Alaska

People ask me, "Aren't you lonely?" Well, there's a million miles of difference between being alone — and being lonely. I think a lot of people just can't take being alone with themselves.

— FRANCES ZAUNMILLER WISNER
Nez Perce Indian, Salmon River Breaks Primitive Area

My father was given ten names to ensure his position in the village. When he was born they called him Tahayghen. The last name they gave him was "nang kwiigee tlaa ahls" (one who is tenfold precious).

— FLORENCE DAVIDSON
Haida Nation, Alaska

There is an old Chinese belief that when the baby begins to smile he is becoming a person. That smile is telling for it reveals a sense of self and a feeling of well-being and intactness.

— GEZA ROHEIM
The Panic of the Gods

Nowadays a lot of the young people are very mixed up about life. I can blame it on different people, on the government, and so on. But mostly it's up to themselves.... The young people who are lost — I hope some day they wake up and realize the evil in their ways. All this alcohol, drugs, and different relationships doesn't lead to happy life.

— BEVERLY HUNGRY WOLF
Blood Indian Reserve, Canada

Everyone hunts for power. Some search for it through control of others. Some look in control of themselves. Some in righteousness. Others in magic. Almost nobody finds its hiding place.

— DOMANO HETAKA
Brazilian Indian, western Amazon basin

Can we ever arrive at any satisfactory knowledge of what constitutes human nature?

— PAUL RADIN
Anthropologist

If you're trying to become a part of a higher expression, don't worry about praise. Don't worry about blame. They'll both trap you. They'll both grind your ass in the ground.

— LEANDIS
Mexican healer, northern Mexico

Perfection is for the gods to achieve. Foolish of me to try to emulate them.

— GUSTI NYOMAN LEMPAD
Balinese artist, teacher

What we do have to learn is to respect ourselves. So many people don't like themselves. They are always trying to change themselves into something else that they see on television. Slim and trim — everyone is dieting. In Somalia they're starving, but here in America people spend millions on diets when they could just shut their mouths.

— JANET MCCLOUD
Tulalip tribe, Washington state

Never spend time with people who don't respect you.

— MAORI PROVERB

Dengan hormat — "With respect."

— INDONESIAN GREETING

I learned to appreciate cooperation in nature and with my fellow men early in life. I felt very much a part of the world and our way of life. I knew I had a place in it, and I felt good about it.

— JOSEPH SUINA
Pueblo, village of Cochiti, New Mexico

GOING WITHIN

So now you want to know some things. Where do you start? That's a good question for you to answer. Maybe just listen. Listen to the drum. Listen to the air. Listen to the breathing...to the earth breathing. Listen to the stars go across the sky.

— MASANEA
Kickapoo, northern Mexico

We have begun a spiritual journey. People want to go back to find the missing link, that hole in their being. They want to fill it with all the possibilities of what we can be.

— CAROLE ANNE HEART LOOKING HORSE
Rosebud/Yankton Sioux from South Dakota

You scream, "I need," and the supply's already here. But if you don't know what the fruit looks like, you could starve to death in a garden.

— LEANDIS
Mexican healer, northern Mexico

Young white kids come to me, New Age kids, and oh god, I love them, but sometimes they are a handful. They come to me and say,

"Oh, Janet, please, please, you got to help me. I've got to get back to nature." I say, "Do you need a laxative, or what?" That's crazy, how can you get back to nature? We *are* nature! We are a part of nature, we are part of this earth, we are a part of everything that lives. We are a part of you and me and this air that connects us all together. There is no esoteric chant or mantra or anything that's going to give these New Agers instant spiritualization. "Give me a pill, give me a chant, I need to be spiritual, right now!" I say you have to learn to be a human being first. If you don't know how to be a human being, you'll never be spiritual.

— JANET MCCLOUD
Tulalip tribe, Washington state

Quiet down, that's when you can think. If you don't, you'll miss everything that was said to you because your mind was involved with what you thought you already knew. Learn to listen. Hear with your heart.

— LEANDIS
Mexican healer, northern Mexico

Give a people a center, and they stand fast.

— MANUEL ELIZALDE JR.
Panamin, Philippines

Meditation is much a part of my being... which, I now understand, is allowing what is so to pour forth from within one's self. It's not from you, but for you. The more I can sit and still myself, to allow the answers to come from within rather than from me dictating what I want and what I need, the more I come to understand my Dodahs [teachers].

— SARA SMITH
Mohawk Tribe, Iroquois Confederacy

Our dream wanderers can direct our way not only through the forest, but also at the major crossroads of our inner lives. Most of us spend our lives wandering throughout amongst the roots of the world — but our dream wanderers, once awakened, can move amongst the upper branches of the Tree of Life, encompassing all things.

— NANYET
High Priest
Punan, Borneo, Indonesia
"Dream wanderer" — intuitive knowing

Life is a ceremony. The Cree teachings are very strong about this. So that when you wake up in the morning, that's a ceremony of life, coming out of the dream-world. When you go into sleep, you're in the dream-world, and you're in a different state of being. Waking up is the ceremony.

— VERNON HARPER
Northern Cree, Canada

We have to learn to see the beauty of the teachings in our dreams, and let them become our guides. It's like us walking on this pathway. We know goodness is there, but we do not always know how to find it. It's when we begin to examine and turn things around to see the many facets both in life and in dreams that we can appreciate the beauty that is within.

— SARA SMITH
Mohawk Tribe, Iroquois Confederacy

It is good that you have questions. Concentrate, look around you, the answer is there.

— TULKU TSEWANG
Cliff dweller, Nepal's remote Dolpo district

One day I asked my mother, "Mom, where's my dreaming place?"
And she took me up in the hills and showed me a waterfall. "That's
your dreaming place," she told me. "When you die you'll go back in
there. And you'll be there forever. You'll be in that waterfall, watching the seasons come and go like your spiritual ancestors. In that
spot, you will be part of the land." That is why we teach you not to
harm or even mark the land. That would be like getting a knife and
cutting yourself.

— PAULINE GORDON
Aboriginal, Bunjalung tribe, Australia

You may travel all over the world and obtain a knowledge of spiritual matters, but you can only find your own spirituality in your own
land. That's where your world started, and that's where your roots
are. Even medicine people can only help where their people are,
where they come from. They have a connection there. That's the way
it is. Always has been.

— LEANDIS
Mexican healer, northern Mexico

A tiger's stripes are on the outside; human stripes are on the inside.

— LADAKHI SAYING
N.E. Kashmir, Indian-Tibetan border

I made it through the sixties, and I told my auntie, "I've made it
through. I'm not going to drink again, and my life is going to
change, but what a waste." But she said, "Vernon, it's like this — life
is like a garden, and for anything to be worthwhile and grow or
bloom, or be productive or beautiful, it takes a lot of shit and a lot
of manure." And that's what I went through. She said, "Now it's up

to you. You can stay in that manure, and you can feel sorry for yourself, or you can grow and bloom into something very beautiful and very productive — it's up to you." Right away I realized she was saying that it wasn't all wasted time.

— VERNON HARPER
Northern Cree, Canada

It's what's awakened inside you that gets interesting, much more interesting than impressing the world, or even yourself.

— DYNAMO JACK
Java native, Indonesia

I live up in Big Cove....I walk up in the mountains, looking for stone and just listening. I get most of my ideas up there and from what my grandpa used to tell me. I use knives. I don't own any power tools. You can't do the detail with power tools, and you rush it and make mistakes. Everything comes from the stone, and you have to let it tell you what it wants you to do. When I am working, I can feel it talking to me. Mostly it comes to me at night. I work from about 12 at night until I get finished, sometimes in an hour or two and sometimes not until dawn. I know when it is finished because the stone won't let me do any more.

— ROBERT AMMONS MANEY
Cherokee, carver of green soapstone

When you adore a statue, you see the carved wood, but you do not see the spirit within; equally, you see the heavens, but nobody has ever seen him who is inside.

— VINCENT GUERRY
Baule descendant, Ivory Coast

No one saw Him, but I think that someone must have seen Him, or we should never have known of Him.

— YUKI INDIAN
Yreka and north Sonoma County, California

How can we know? We can't see him; perhaps only when we die will we know and then we can't tell anyone. So how can we say what he is like or what his name is? But he must be good to give us so many things. He must be of the forest. So when we sing, we sing to the forest.

— MOKE
Ituri Forest dweller, Democratic Republic of Congo, Africa,
In response to identifying a supreme power

The different religions confused me. Which was the right one? I tried to figure it out but had no success. It worried me. The different Gods — Catholic, Jewish, Protestant, Mohammedan — seemed all very particular in the way in which they expected me to keep on good terms with them. I couldn't please one without offending the others. One kind soul solved my problem by taking me on my first trip to the planetarium. I contemplated the insignificant flyspeck called earth, the millions of suns and solar systems, and concluded that whoever was in charge of all this would not throw a fit if I ate ham, or meat on Friday, or did not fast in the daytime during Ramadan. I felt much better after this.

— JOHN (FIRE) LAME DEER
Lakota

There is a church on one of the islands, three hours away by boat. But is that too long a trip for a chance to talk with God?

— AYMARA INDIAN
Altiplano Island, tennis-court size island off of Peru

In 1976, when I was in Maui giving a talk at Hawaii University, I went to the beach one day wearing a hat and boots. . . . I noticed some people sitting in a circle staring at me, especially one young man with very bushy, long hair and a full beard. After a while he motioned to me to come over, I obliged. They were passing around this short little stub of a cigarette and sucking away on it. I didn't know anything about marijuana at the time, so I thought, these guys are really poor. They're even poorer than I am, to suck away on a little bitty stub. . . . The bushy one asked me where I was from, and I told him I was an Oglala medicine man from the Pine Ridge reservation. He said, "I had a vision. In this vision I've seen God, and he spoke to me and I spoke to him." That got me mad. . . . I told him, "If you'd really seen God, and he'd spoken to you, you would not be here. You would be walking the highway trying to save souls, preaching his words, and healing the sick." He didn't answer me, and I walked away.

— PETE CATCHES
Lakota elder, Oglala holy man

Now if someone says to me, "I'm not spiritual," I'll say, "You breathe, don't you?" Well, that's spiritual. Spirituality is breath, and you take it from there.

— VERNON HARPER
Northern Cree, Canada

We do not call out to God by name. We do this [deep inhalation], and that is God.

— DAVID BURGOS
Mayan, Muna, Yucatan

If you were to tell me that you were getting sick, and asked me, "Grandmother, teach me how to pray," I would ask, "What have you been doing to yourself that is making you sick?" Then I would tell you how to pray in order to understand yourself. I would tell you, for the next eleven days, take a glass of water and something from your own culture to bless it with — for us it's sweet grass, cedar, or sage — then bless the water and pray early in the morning before the sun comes. That way you will make your connection with the Creator at that same time for eleven mornings. If you miss one morning, then you have to start over and keep going until you complete the eleven days. By that time you will be in touch with the Creator and also in touch with your own self — and your own spirit.

— ROSE AUGER
Woodland Cree, Canada

When we sang our praises to the sun or the moon or wind, you said we were worshipping idols. Without understanding, you condemned us as lost souls just because our form of worship was different from yours. We saw the Great Spirit's work in almost everything: sun, moon, trees, wind, and mountains. Sometimes we appreciated him through these things. Was that so bad? I think we have a true belief in the supreme being, a stronger faith than that of most whites who have called us pagans.

— TATANGA MANI (WALKING BUFFALO)
Stoney Indian, Alberta, Canada

Spirituality is what holds the world and mankind together. When it's gone, there is nothing. Like a dead person when their spirit leaves them.

— BERTHA GROVE
Southern Ute Indian Reservation, Colorado

THE SOWER
of CIRCUMSTANCES

FORGED ENDURANCE

There are no secrets. In time, everything will be known. Nothing can be hidden. Your life is written as you live it. You write it yourself, and it goes in front of you. Those who can see, know you...know who you are, what you have done. There's no right and wrong, just what you have done to create the situations you need. It's up to you to learn and change. If you don't change, you just keep having lessons.

— LEANDIS
Mexican healer, northern Mexico

Life always creates difficulties. You must move forward and not be afraid to make mistakes. But don't allow mistakes to go on too long. And don't cover up the difficulties.

— BAC HO
Vietnamese, Vietnam

Write the wrongs that are done to you in sand, but write the good things that happen to you on a piece of marble. Let go of all emotions such as resentment and retaliation, which diminish you, and hold onto the emotions, such as gratitude and joy, which increase you.

— ARABIC SAYING

When you can see, just give thanks for what you have gone through, what you are going through. Just give thanks. When you start doing that, things will change.... You may think you have lost everything, but when you can see you will know you have gained more than you ever had to give up. You will have found yourself. Some never do.

— LEE LYONS
Onondaga Nation

I had accepted a lot of challenges over the years, and I was always somehow able to overcome them. But I met more than I could manage with alcohol and drugs. For three years, I was a drunk.... Maybe I had to suffer, maybe I was meant to experience the depths of self-pity and low self-esteem in order to understand that I never want my children to have to go through this. I want to see my children free to pursue happiness, education, and career opportunities. I want them to develop good relationships with people their own age and, of course, with the elders.

— MIKE HANEY
Lakota/Seminole

The past may become either an opportunity or an obstacle. Everything depends on what we make of it and not what it makes of us.

— SARVEPALLI RADHAKRISHNAN
India

We have been told so many times that we are low that it is carved on our brains, like the carpenter carves on wood.

— SAIFULLAH
Kalash tribesman, Pakistan

Listen. We're not being punished. We're being given opportunities. The bad things that happen to us in this life are not punishment.

Punishment is the idea, "If it's painful, I'm bad and I'm being punished." This is not punishment. The one thing that the Creator cannot forgive us of is condemning ourselves because he didn't condemn us.... Condemnation is our idea.

— LEANDIS
Healer, Northern Mexico

There was a time in my life I felt so low, I started drinking for about two weeks straight. I was alone, I didn't want to talk to anyone. I remember one night I was so drunk I took off and didn't remember anything. Next thing I knew I was lying inside a car, the car I had just wrecked. I felt my body packed in the car, so squashed I was barely able to breathe. I squeezed my way through a little opening and got out. I remembered I was mad, thinking I wasn't ready to die. The next day there were cuts, and I was squeezing glass from my skin. I went into the sweat lodge and prayed. I decided then I'd be a stronger person. That was in 1988. Since then I stopped drinking.

— ARVOL LOOKING HORSE
Keeper of the Pipe, Lakota

Without the breakdowns in your life, you wouldn't have the whole picture. There's a purpose in everything. Don't go out and hang yourself because of a lesson.... Go below the surface, go deeper. Remember, you get what you ask for. Don't let your lessons destroy you or you'll miss the point, and you'll miss out on what the Creator had prepared for you.

— LEANDIS
Healer, Northern Mexico

We must take risks and deal directly with life's hardships, in order to regain our identity and spirituality. We must release the trauma. Then mothers will begin to see their sons for the first time, sons will see their fathers for the first time. Then, we can all go home again, become families and villages.

— HAROLD NAPOLEON
Yup'ik, Paimute, Alaska

I have gone through some pretty traumatic challenges.... But the greatest challenge I had was when I had to face the possibility of losing a child, not once, but twice. Then it was always that inner voice that spoke to me and told me that these children are not your children, they are a gift to you to be cherished for only so long. Be grateful for the time you've had with them, to care and to comfort and carry them in your heart forever. These experiences made me become stronger in my beliefs.

— SARA SMITH
Mohawk Tribe, Iroquois Confederacy

If a man loses his wife, his friends come and help him cry. He cries for four days, but no longer, because life must go on, and if he cries too much the spirits will give him something extra to cry about.

— JOHN (FIRE) LAME DEER
Lakota

In your heart, your child, your mother, and your father are all equal. When any one of them dies, your heart feels pain. When your child dies, you think, "How come this little thing I held beside me and watched all that she did, today has died and left me?" ... You cry out ... and cry and cry and cry. It is the same if it is your mother. You cry for her as you do for your child. You pull off your beads and ornaments so your neck and body are bare.... Your thoughts come from your heart.... Perhaps your father is still alive and living with you. But after time passes, his months are also finished.... Who's going to help me now?... You cry and mourn for your father, cry and cry and cry. Finally people tell you, "Look even if you continue to cry like this, where do you think your father is? Where do you think you are going to see him?...If you keep crying like this, God will take you, too, and then you will be able to see him. How else will your crying help you to see him again?" Soon, you are quiet. You finish mourning and just sit. It's the same for your husband.

— NISA
Kung! woman, Kalahari Desert, Botswana

In our language there's a word, "nhebasu." It's a word that covers a lot of things that the white man's language doesn't. The white man has sadness, despair, difficulty, but "nhebasu" is more than that.

— SALVADOR SANCHEZ
Guarani-Kaiowa Indian, southwestern Brazil

Do not grieve. Misfortunes will happen to the wisest and best of men. Death will come and always out of season. It is the command of the Great Spirit, and all nations and people must obey. What is past and cannot be prevented should not be grieved for....Misfortunes do not flourish particularly in our path. They grow everywhere.

— BIG ELK
Omaha, funeral oration

We're not sugar. We won't melt.

— VIKTOR KORZHAVIN
Villager, Avdotino, Russia,
Expressing his attitude about meeting adversity in life

I have not let myself fall into despair, even when the news has not been what I hoped for. I just put one foot in front of the other and keep moving and am grateful for each day.

— WILMA MANKILLER
Cherokee Nation Chief, 1985–1995

Don't expect anything to be good or bad. Everything just is. That's the way creation works. Right now, this is how "it" appears to you. So if you want it different, the only thing to do is see it different.

— LEANDIS
Healer, Northern Mexico

One of the things that I find is that people will fall back on how they were raised and what happened to them, saying, Well, my father was a cruel man, and I have low self-esteem, and I can't comprehend what you are teaching me about love and kindness and giving. And I say, Do not fall back on that kind of garbage. The Creator gave you a sound mind and an incredible spirit and a way of being so that you can do anything right now! You can change that attitude same as you wake up in the morning and it's a new day. Your mind and everything else can be new. I've lived through hardships and horror, and I'm a loving, caring, and giving person because I choose to be that way. I choose to listen to the other side to guide me. We all have the ability with our spirit to change things right now.

— ROSE AUGER
Woodland Cree, Canada

Everybody has his own problems. Big people have big problems and small people have small problems.

— VISHNU MAYA
Gurung tribe, central Nepal

My strength was not much, but I began the up-river journey at once, and I sang to the dogs as they ran strongly to the west.... Two days up river and a few miles north of my track was a lake and by it two camps where I had stopped overnight on my way to the sea. In those camps I had been given soup made of old bones by people who were almost old bones themselves. Now, with much food on my sled, I did not turn off to give them at least a little of my meat and fat. I told myself I could spare neither the time nor the food if I was to save my own family from death...but I knew I did wrong...if only I had...but such thoughts are useless, and they are a weakness in man; for he does what he does, and he must pay what he pays.

— ANOTEELIK
Inuit, Hudson Bay, Canada

You have shadows, but shadows are only the dark side of experiences to which you have attached emotions. Go back, take away the emotions, learn from the experiences, and pure reason returns. With perfect reason comes intuition. With perfect intuition comes a complete understanding and peace....If it was not for the experiences, even the ones with shadows, you would not be where you are now. They will help you get to where you are supposed to be.

— LEANDIS
Mexican healer, northern Mexico

If you cannot bear the smoke, you will never get to the fire.

— WODAABE SAYING
Nomads in the sub-Saharan terrain of Niger

There was a good little frog, reasonable and well adjusted to reality who, hopping around minding her own business, accidentally fell into a bucket of milk. Appraising the situation, she soon realized the physical impossibility of her jumping out again to save herself because of the size and the bucket. Accepting the inevitable, she promptly drowned. The following day another innocent little frog made the same mistake and fell into a similar bucket equal in size and filled with milk. This little frog, however, was totally unreasonable, impulsive, and unrealistic. She jumped and jumped and never gave up jumping until the following day at dawn; after having churned the milk into solid butter by her ceaseless jumping, she was saved.

— ROMA STORY

I forbid you to become discouraged.

— BHUMIBOL ADULYADEJ
Thai native, Thailand

WORKING IT OUT

My parents had what is called "gaman" — inner strength, the strength to persevere. It's a great legacy for us.

— JUNKOH HARUI
Puget Sound islander

Now I remembered how Mama had fought for a roof over her children's heads; she was the model I worked from. The kids and I climbed the steps notched into the mountain to a field that was bald except for a single clump of eucalyptus trees. Other people were arriving with their belongings. I set down my mattress and put the pots under a bush. We picked up rocks and sticks and began to build our house.... We were making something for ourselves. Three days later, when our shack was finished, the kids and I stood on the road below, gazing up at it. We looked at it to make sure it existed. "You remember before?" I said to the kids. "When we didn't have a house, only this mattress in your grandma's room? Then you found sticks and bricks to make our new house strong. When you grow up, I want you to be independent. This shack is a lesson. When you're older, we'll have more things, better things. But it's good to build in stages."

— ALICIA VÁSQUEZ
Born in the village of Pan de Azúcar, Colombian Andes, South America

If you are idle now, you will be idle forever.

— ZULU ELDER
South Africa

The Basques do not have much use for those who won't do their duty. They censure them with silence or forget they exist. On the surface these may seem hard terms for living, but you must remember that this is a people who could not have survived as a race without the most rigid rules of group conduct.

— JEAN MIRANDE
Commenting on the Basque of the Pyrenees

We work as hard as you do. Did you ever try skinning a buffalo?

— OURAY
Ute, Colorado

They say that if you work too hard you'll die early and if you sleep too much you'll die early. I do both too much and can't understand why I'm not dead yet.

— VISHNU MAYA
Gurung tribe, central Nepal

Human beings must have challenge! That is understood by any thinking person, and we know the best challenge is the one which is the most natural. If men do not have such challenge, they find it in unnatural ways — perhaps in a fierce competition for power or money, perhaps in internal struggles that tear a society apart, perhaps in external struggles that become bloody wars. We know all this, you see; and so we have deliberately offered to our people — particularly the young — the challenge of the North, which is a challenge of nature. They have responded with enthusiasm. It is not good to give people security of body alone...we must also make a valid and good purpose for life. Those who go North find such a purpose.

— YOUNG SIBERIAN WOMAN
On the northern region of Chernychevsky, Siberia

If you survive here, you are entitled to live by your own standards.

— DORIS SAUNDERS
Labradorian, Canada

To strengthen myself, I spend time five days a week working out in a weight room that I built. I find the exercises to be a strain. My muscles hurt, and I am sometimes forced to gasp for air. So it is with my people. As we advance deeper into the modern world, we stretch our abilities and it hurts. Some see us struggling for a deeper breath and think we are drowning. Yet, when I recover from a workout, I feel much stronger and am able to do even more than before. So it will be with my Apache people.

— RONNIE LUPE
White Mountain Apache
Fort Apache Reservation, Arizona

Learn to work. Let us work together.... Then when I die, you will know how to work.... So let us work well and eat well while we live. When we work, we work until midafternoon. When you are young, you want to work all day. But I tell you, "Enough, enough. It is very late. We have to return to the house, and you have to bathe. Then let us eat well."

— JIVARO NATIVE OF EASTERN ECUADOR
Talking to his son

THE EASY LIFE

I can't understand it. My sister in the capital, she now has all these things that do the work faster. She just buys her clothes in a shop, she has a jeep, a telephone, a gas cooker. All of these things save so much time, and yet when I go to visit her, she doesn't have time to talk to me.

— LADAKHI VILLAGER
N.E. Kashmir, Indian-Tibetan border

Today, the younger generation has more knowledge of the outside. Fewer and fewer are looking to the land. They are dreaming of how to get money in their pockets. I am trying to think ahead, to see what we can do to match the times.

— CHIEF TAUILI'ILI
Island of Ofu, Samoa

When you pray, don't ask for worldly things — money, riches, or luck — don't ask for that, because the Old Man won't listen.

— WILLARD RHOADES
Achumawi band, Pit River tribe

Many people have money, but they are unhappy. They always want more. Sometimes having wealth makes the mind poor. And being poor makes the mind rich.

— VIETNAMESE VILLAGER

The Gaje [non-Gypsies] constantly wish that things were different. In summer they want snow and in winter sunshine. Don't they realize that you cannot buy what is not for sale?

— BELGIAN ROMANI BOY, AGE TEN

And your Las Vegas. It's like a cold shower. It makes the blood circulate, but you cannot stay in the shower forever.... Here we do not sell noises or neon signs. We have a different merchandise — solitude, sun, peace, pure air.

FRANCISCO ARAMBURO
Native of La Paz, Baja

We may not have automobiles, juke boxes, or Coca-Cola, but here a man lives close to the soil. That, señor, is where God meant him to be.

— MIGUEL CASTILLO
Mountain farmer from Los Nevados, Venezuela

Bad roads, good people. Good roads, all kinds of people.

— DOÑA ANITA ESPINOZA
Elderly matriarch of El Rosario, Baja California
On developed roadways

We don't have any cars here. I can offer you only one horse, and he is dangerous.

— FERNANDO ROJAS GALLARDO
Villager, San Juan Bautista, Isla Robinson Crusoe, Chile

An easy life doesn't teach you how to live.

— ALICIA VÁSQUEZ
Born in the village of Pan de Azúcar, Colombian Andes, South America

Samuel Wassilie came in one day worried about the young kids going off on snowmobiles because the machines often break down. So he took the whole class out in the woods, cut down a tree, and showed them how to make snowshoes for an emergency.

— DON KINSEY
Eskimo teacher at Aleknagik, Alaska
On an elder's concern for the younger generation

Sure! Ask them to saddle a horse, they put it on backwards. Ask them to yoke a dzo [cross between a cow and a yak], they run away scared. They buy expensive rubber boots that fall apart before you get to the top of the pass. We wore shoes we made ourselves that were warm and comfortable, and carried needle and thread and could repair anything we needed in a minute. We stood on our own two legs and knew how to make use of everything around us.

— ELDER LADAKHI
Upbraiding Ladakhi youth
N.E. Kashmir, Indian-Tibet border

Czechs may have more automobiles, but we have more fun out of life.

— STEFAN GÁL
Slovak, Slovak Republic

I think people everywhere have gifts and wisdom, but today many cultures are lost in the haste of a materialistic world.

— PAULINE TANGIORA
Maori native, New Zealand

The open air is the place for a man, not the smoke of towns.

— MOHAMMED NAIM
Villager, Garmsel, Afghanistan

"Watch the ashes, don't smoke, you stain the curtains. Watch the goldfish bowl, don't breathe on the parakeet, don't lean your head against the wallpaper; your hair may be greasy. Don't spill liquor on that table: it has a delicate finish. You should have wiped your boots; the floor was just varnished. Don't, don't, don't..." That is crazy. We weren't made to endure this. You live in prisons which you have built for yourselves, calling them "homes," offices, factories. We have a new joke on the reservation: "What is cultural deprivation?" Answer: "Being an upper-middle class white kid in a split-level suburban home with a color TV."

— JOHN (FIRE) LAME DEER
Sioux medicine man

Everybody seems to want to make money and have a nice car. That's the thought, so how are you going to win? Nobody wants to start walking, but they're doing a lot of running for exercise.

— LEON SHENANDOAH
Onondaga Nation, Nedrow, New York

In the old days, we had to make ourselves better. Now we have doctors and nurses to make us better.

— ANN MEEKITJUK HANSON
Inuit, Nunavut ("our land"), Canada

Our Indian people didn't believe in being overweight....It was like committing a sin if you let yourself get fat. It meant you weren't taking care of your body. Because you were never supposed to put anything in your body that was going to harm it. And you never overate. You were to take a mouthful of food and put your spoon down until you swallow it, and then you just sit there and wait a little bit and take another spoonful.

— GEORGIANA TRULL
Yurok Nation, Klamath River, northern California

Life is easier now, but not as satisfying.

— JOE FRIDAY
Yup'ik, Chevak, Alaska

Wow! People were amazed that somebody could receive money for doing nothing.

— ANN MEEKITJUK HANSON
Inuit, Nunavut ("our land"), Canada,
On welfare, called "waiting" by the Inuit

People live out of a can. They need to know the way we lived before, the way things taste from nature.

— BONIFACIO MONTOYA
Villager in El Ancon, New Mexico

Hunzakuts don't mind feeding the myth that they live longer than anybody else in the world, attributing it to their "pure" diet, which, they claim, became corrupted when the British introduced "the five adulterants" — sugar, tobacco, spices, tea, and vegetable oil — into their mountain fastness.

— JOHN MCCARRY
"High Road to Hunza," Hunza, high glaciers of Pakistan

I do not think I could live as you do — it is too demanding. You are always under pressure because you must compete. You must make as much money as you can because you pay for so many things that should be free.

— SIBERIAN VILLAGER ON THE RIVER OB

My son is civilized. He eats with a spoon, and pees standing.

— ELDERLY VILLAGER
Qabab, Iraq
On her son in Amara

My father learned the lessons of life personally from his father, whereas I took them from books, magazines, and television. My wife, instead of listening to her mother about baby feeding, learned from Dr. Spock's bestseller. We are the first generation with this new source of knowledge — the mass media.

— LEE SOO JIN
Singapore

If we do not want to sacrifice too many of our old values on the altar of modernization, then we should be more careful about equating quality with quantity, of pricing people's worth according to their possessions.

— JANE DAKUVULU
Fiji Islander

We are still reaching for the sky. In the developed countries, people are coming back down, saying, "It's empty up there."

— GYELONG PALDAN
Ladakhi, N.E. Kashmir, Indian-Tibetan border

You could take the paved highway, but the old road is better, when the moon permits.

— BAJO Y AFUERA
Villager, Ecuador

I say to my country and to other developing countries, that in our race to modernize, we must respect the rich ancient cultures and traditions of our peoples. We must not blindly follow the model of progress invented by Western civilization. We may envy the industrialized world for its wealth, but we must not forget that this world was bought at a very high price. The rich world suffers so much stress, pollution, violence, poverty, and spiritual emptiness. The riches of indigenous communities lie not in money or commodities, but in community, in tradition, and the sense of belonging to a special place.

— MUTANG URUD
Kelabit tribesman, Sarawak, Malaysia, island of Borneo

THE DRUMMER
of STILLNESS

HARMONY IN MOTION

Man can, my people believe, exercise some control over the orderly rhythm of the world with his actions, thoughts, emotions, and will. Man must, to avoid failure, see the world whole and understand the relationship of all that goes to make up the harmonious ebb and flow, the decay and creation.

— NAQUIMA
Hopi, in drama "Desert Soliloquy" by Len Peterson

We direct to your mind that peace is not merely the absence of war, but the constant effort to maintain harmonious existence between peoples, from individual to individual and between humans and the other beings of this planet. We point out to you that a Spiritual Consciousness is the Path to Survival of Humankind. We who walk about on Mother Earth occupy this place for only a short time. It is our duty as human beings to preserve the life that is here for the benefit of the generations yet unborn.

— PASSAGE FROM THE SIX NATIONS IROQUOIS CONFEDERACY
Statement to the World, May 1979

With Harmony may I walk. With Harmony behind me, may I walk. With Harmony above me, may I walk. With Harmony below me, may I walk. With Harmony all around me, may I walk.... It is finished in Harmony. It is finished in Harmony.

— NAVAJO "NIGHTWAY CHANT"

Qunnikun, qunnikun — "Give us smooth water."

— NETSILIK SAYING
Northern Canada

Where I come from we say that rhythm is the soul of life because the whole universe revolves around rhythm; and when we get out of rhythm, that's when we get into trouble. For this reason the drum, next to the human voice, is our most important instrument. It is special.

— BABATUNDE OLATUNJI
Nigerian drummer

We sang songs that carried in their melodies all the sounds of nature — the running of waters, the sighing of winds, and the calls of the animals. Teach these to your children that they may come to love nature as we love it.

— GRAND COUNCIL FIRE OF AMERICAN INDIANS, 1927

It took me so long to learn this song, and this thing has learned it at once without making any mistakes!

— GILYAK WOMAN
Siberia, speaking about a tape recorder

The long song sings about the expanse of Mongolia. . . . The long song sings about the steppes and about life being a very broad, a very wide experience. But people can only think of their horses galloping through life. Every song is about this wonderful horse, flying against the wind like a bird....For Mongolians, a person who cannot play a morin khour [stringed instrument] or sing a song is not a human being.

— OYUN, MONGOLIAN STORYTELLER
Nomadic culture, Mongolian steppes

In Africa, it is said that "If you can talk, you can sing; if you can walk, you can dance."

— ANGELES ARRIEN
Cultural anthropologist

Reasoning about God and other ethics came late. Primitive man sought his answers in myth and ritual; he danced out his faith before he thought it out.

— DR. HUSTON SMITH
Great Religions of the World

One slave girl brought that little five-line song with her. They took everything she had but her dignity, and they couldn't take the song.

— MARY MORAN
African-American from Georgia
On her grandmother who came from Sierra Leone, Africa,
Bringing with her a song of the Mende people

Ota's moonlight dances were not excuses for silliness, loudness, or any old gyrations. There was a right way to move, there was stillness and silence beneath the chant. There was energy and discipline all at once, even the suggestion of religion.

— OTA BENGA
Mbuti, Kasai River, South Central Africa

When I talked to a noted Lakota dancer about the unusual design of his regalia, I expected a description of history and research. He said:

"It came in a vision." I had a sudden image of a way of life whose surface is less solid than my own, a life in which you can see through the skin of the earth and time, as if it were only painted gauze, to the texture of the past and the visions beyond it. Indians scatter litter on the surface as if they don't care, but they attend carefully to the layers they see on the other side. No wonder music and dance, those tools we use to reach beyond words, are so important.

— MICHAEL PARFIT
"Powwow — A Gathering of the Tribes"

Mother is smaller than she used to be. I am taller than she is, much taller. Her voice is soft like the big gray duck which comes only in the moons of the harvest. It says, sho, sho, sho. Grandmother told Tushi it was my father who gave Mother the name Wakara — Full Moon — because, he said, she moves in quietness as does the moon.

— ISHI
Last of the Yahi tribe, western foothills of Mount Lassen
Recounting his childhood

The dances show the beauty and the soft side of human being. The girls...their personality changed. They're softer, more feminine, more woman-like. The boys, they're more kind. It's showing the gentle side of them.

— SEAN MERA OU
Cambodian

We are adding new dances all the time, using the old songs.... We just go by the little knowledge people gave us and make up the rest. You can tell, when you are doing a new or different dance, whether it works or not. It is like getting in the car and driving: You can drive if you don't hit anything; but if you start hitting things, it doesn't work.

— REGGIE DAVIDSON
Haida Nation, Alaska

When you are at the potlatch [Haida celebration] and you feel the song is just right, and the dancer is doing it just right, and everybody is right into it, and they are focused on it, they can't take their eyes off it, and their heart just swells, and you find it in your throat, and you know that you could close your eyes and still feel it — that's what you are there to do, to share that feeling with the people. To strive for that harmony and unity is how you learn to be a correct human being.

— JOE DAVID
Haida Nation, Alaska

That's how we are, we Juchitecas, the rain may be falling, but we are still dancing.

— JUCHITAN NATIVE
The "Cloud People," Zapotec, Mexico

I don't think we could manage a real riot. Someone would be bound to start playing a ukulele, and that would be the end of it.

— YOUNG RAROTONGAN
Rarotonga, Cook Islands

"The whole world must work in harmony, Naquima. Nature, the gods, the plants, the animals, and men need each other and must work together for the good of all. There is no place for selfish men, or even for a selfish man among men; it would throw everything out of balance and endanger the whole universe. To be a good Hopi, Naquima, you will work for the good of your family, your clan, the village...." Naquima: "And the whole world."

— HOPI FATHER AND SON TALKING IN THE DRAMA
"Desert Soliloquy" by Len Peterson

Peace be unto this house, and peace be with all who dwell herein. Let harmony be forever here, and let love abound.

— ROMA PROVERB
Hungary

Hagosheen — "Fine with me."

— NAVAJO SAYING

We must learn to live in harmony...we have common enemies to fight together: ignorance, fear, hatred, and violence.

— BEMNAL BHIKKHU
Buddhist monk
Chakma tribe, Chittagong Hill Tract, Bangladesh

RIDING IT OUT

Mañana, horita — "Tomorrow and in a little hour, all will be done."
— YUCATEC SAYING
Yucatan, Mexico

Sumatra taught me many things, but perhaps the most useful was the humbling concept of "jam karet" — rubber time. It has nothing to do with rubber trees, though that vast Indonesian island taps more than its share of them. No, "jam karet" has to do with filtering frustration out of daily events and accepting what must be.
— HARVEY ARDEN
"A Sumatran Journey," Indonesia's Sumatra

Ajornarmat — "That's life."

— ESKIMO SAYING
Eastern Arctic

I shrugged my shoulders and muttered, "Iyonamut." This word expresses the philosophy of the Eskimo, his patient courage in the face of long, long odds against him. It means something like, "It can't be helped," or "That's life for you," or "I've done my damnedest and now Fate takes over." It is not so much defeatism as acceptance of the inevitable.

— LEWIS COTLOW
In Search of the Primitive

What happened happened, that's all.

— TECUMSEH DEERFOOT COOK
Pamunkey Indian, Virginia
Reflecting on what happened to his people
with the settlement of Virginia

Take what today brings; as for tomorrow, "jes hol' strain" — relax.

— SAYING OF THE GRENADINE ISLANDS

This is how they work. Inuit don't have to get an acknowledgment of a win or loss in discussion. They just float an idea and sit back.

— CANADIAN BUREAUCRAT
Iqaluit, Canada

Mana e ndina — "So be it."

— SAYING OF THE FIJI ISLANDERS

THE FORAGER
of AWARENESS

NESTLED IN NATURE

Sit down on the dirt here and lean back on the rock. Get comfortable....Fill yourself completely with the life that is around you.

— DOMANO HETAKA
Brazilian Indian, western Amazon basin

Every time you admire something in nature, it's a prayer to the Creator.

— VERNON HARPER
Northern Cree, Canada

I still pray to the streams, to the mountains. I sing the old songs. I offer my sacrifices to the corn. Not only for myself, but for my children and grandchildren and for all people.

— ROBERTA BLACKGOAT
Navajo, Big Mountain, Arizona

Others may laugh at our customs and how we are so closely related to the land and all things that grow on the land. But all the trees, animals, fish, insects, reptiles, and even mountains have special meaning for us.

— WEST PAPUAN ELDER
Papua New Guinea

We believe every little thing in our environment is connected. For example, the elderberry trees told us when it was safe to eat seafood. We knew that from the time the elderberry blooms in spring, to the time it drops its fruit in the fall, you didn't go for shellfish. The elderberry told us through its song when the red tide was in.

— BERNICE TORREZ
Pomo healer, California

The lives of our people are written in the landscape. And we know every tree and turn of the creeks. In cities I get lost easily, but out there in the forest I always know where I am. We have names for thousands of streams and creeks, even the smallest trickles.

— MUTANG URUD
Kelabit tribesman, Borneo, Malay Peninsula

Oh, Yes, I went to the white man's schools. I learned to read from school books, newspapers, and the Bible. But in time I found that these were not enough. Civilized people depend too much on man-made printed pages. I turn to the Great Spirit's book which is the whole of his creation. You can read a big part of that book if you study nature. You know, if you take all your books, lay them out under the sun and let the snow and rain and insects work on them for a while, there will be nothing left. But the Great Spirit has provided you and me with an opportunity for study in nature's university: the forests, the rivers, the mountains, and the animals which include us.

— TATANGA MANI, WALKING BUFFALO
Stoney Indian, Alberta, Canada

I never went to school until I was thirteen, but I learned from living out in the wilderness, our natural world. Right now I can survive in the government world. But I'd rather live in the natural world.

— SARAH JAMES
Gwich'in Indian, Arctic Village

For me, it's important to work the land because she feeds us. I can't imagine any other kind of life.

— PARASKA BODNARUK
Hutsul artist, Kryvorivnya, southwestern Ukraine

Sometimes I feel like the first being in one of our Indian legends. This was a giant made of earth, water, the moon, and the winds. He had timber instead of hair, a whole forest of trees. He had a huge lake in his stomach and a waterfall in his crotch. I feel like this giant. All of nature is in me, and a bit of myself is in all of nature.

— JOHN (FIRE) LAME DEER
Sioux medicine man

When a Karen child is born, the father of the newborn takes the placenta and umbilical cord and walks deep into the forest, where he selects a large tree and offers to it the afterbirth by placing it in the crook of a branch. The tree, which exemplifies both life and longevity, becomes a lifetime reminder to the Karen child that his or her own health and well-being are related to the health and well-being of that tree.... When the child is old enough to walk and understand, the father will guide his daughter or son to the forest to see her or his "life tree" and to know that she or he must nurture and care for this ancient being.

— SERI THONGMAK AND DAVID L. HULSE
"The Winds of Change: Karen People in Harmony with World Heritage"
About the Karen people of the Myanmar and Thailand highlands

We must have trees around us.

— SEMANG TRIBAL SAYING
Malay Peninsula

The land is our provider, our healer, and our inspiration.

— ROBBIE NIQUANICAPPO
Cree Indian, Quebec

Civilized people...do not realize how these people [Romani], who pass half their lives in wild places watching waving grass and falling waters and listening to the brook until its cadence speaks in real song, believe in their inspirations and feel that there is the same mystical feeling and presence in all things that live and move and murmur as well as in themselves.

— CHARLES GODFREY LELAND
Gypsy Sorcery and Fortunetelling

Walking home with Lazaro Pech, I asked him about the Maya houses. He told me that certain woods had to be sought for the building and that the roof has more than four thousand palm leaves in its thatch....I rambled on. "I used to live in France, and I found houses with thatched roofs in Normandy, among the apple orchards. Then there is England, where we had a great poet, Shakespeare. Have you heard of him?" No, Lazaro had not heard of him, or of any poetry except the sound of the wind in the trees and the mysterious ways of the natural life.

— LAWRENCE DAME
Yucatan, Mexico

Let's sit down here, all of us, on the open prairie, where we can't see a highway or a fence. Let's have no blankets to sit on, but feel the ground with our bodies, the earth, the yielding shrubs. Let's have the grass for a mattress, experiencing its hardness and its softness. Let us become like stones, plants, and trees. Let us be animals, think and feel like animals. Listen to the air. You can hear it, feel it, smell it, taste it. "Woniya waken" — the holy air — which renews all by its breath. "Woniya, woniya waken" — spirit, life, breath, renewal — it means all that. "Woniya" — we sit together, don't touch, but something is there; we feel it between us, as a presence.

— JOHN (FIRE) LAME DEER
Sioux medicine man

If you understand the earth, it will understand you.

— ALEXANDER POPROV
Villager, Kuibyshevskoye, Russia, Baltic Sea

The Earth's education is the best form of education. I believe in this story of mothers and fathers, the Mother Earth and my Father in Heaven. I believe this is a way to integrate and guide our lives, a way that could help us unite . . . not just tomorrow or the next day, but far into the future.

— BERITO KUBARUWA
President of the U'wa Traditional Authority, Colombia

Nature herself does not speak with a voice that we can easily understand. Neither can the animals and birds we are threatening with extinction talk to us. Who in this world can speak for nature and the spiritual energy that creates and flows through all life? In every continent are human beings who are like you but who have not separated themselves from the land and from nature. It is through their voice that nature can speak to us.

— THOMAS BANYACYA
Hopi elder, Hotevilla, northern Arizona desert

LISTENING TO NATURE

"Susu mai" — Listen.

— FORMAL SAMOAN GREETING

In the Cree teachings, "The Listening" means more than anything else to us. The Cree Indian people learn how to listen to the environment, to the wind, to the rocks. We learn how to listen to everything. Some of the elders are saying that our young people need help to get back to "The Listening."

— VERNON HARPER
Northern Cree, Canada

Wherever one looks, the life of this world depends on water. But if the water itself feels thirsty, from what well can one quench its thirst?

— SOMALI NOMAD
Ogaden Desert, Africa

My parents taught us to revere and express gratitude to the kamui [spirit] of fire, water, and mountains, in which are found the essentials for our living. We no longer hear the wind, we no longer hear the language of the stones, the colors, any of the forces of nature; we don't tune in to them anymore because we have long closed our ears and allowed them to go to sleep. It's time to wake our own ears up and listen. Every other living thing has maintained and is carrying out their duties and responsibilities; it is we humans who have forgotten to do that. We have taken things for granted. We have used and abused all of the sacred gifts that were put here for our use so that we could learn from them. The elements are our greatest teachers, the wind, the four-leggeds. Each comes to us with its unique teachings. All birds are messengers; they teach us to rise above the situation, to be free and rise above. Right from the tiniest winged ones to the eagle, their message is the same, to rise above situations and be free.

— SARA SMITH
Mohawk Tribe, Iroquois Confederacy

Maybe us Gajos [non-Gypsies] have lived so long in four walls that we've shut out the sound of God's voice, so long under roofs that we can't read the signs in the sky.

— TRAVELING MAN MARRIED TO A ROMA WOMAN

We were never meant to live in houses with walls and built in a square. We were to always remember the circle. Like life. Like the sun. The moon. The earth. Like our time on the earth.

— MASANEA
Kickapoo, northern Mexico,
Nacimiento de los Kickapoo

I think white people are so afraid of the world they created that they don't want to see, feel, smell, or hear it. The feeling of rain and snow on your face, being numbed by an icy wind and thawing out before a smoking fire, coming out of a hot sweat bath and plunging into a cold stream, these things make you feel alive, but you don't want them anymore...living inside a body that no longer has a scent, hearing the noise from the hi-fi instead of listening to the sounds of nature, watching some actor on TV having a make-believe experience when you no longer experience anything for yourself....It's no good.

— JOHN (FIRE) LAME DEER
Sioux medicine man

Yes, many Indian people in Central America are endangered. They need help and they know it. But remember, most people in the Western world are also lost. They have lost their connection with nature, which is essential. How will they be rescued?

— MIGUEL SOTO
Costa Rican Indian, Costa Rica

It's amazing how indirect everything is here. They write about the beauty of nature, they talk about it, and everywhere there are potted plants and plastic plants, and pictures of trees on the wall. And all the time television programs about nature. But they don't ever seem to have contact with the real thing.

— TASHI RABGYA
Ladakhi, N.E. Kashmir Indian-Tibetan border
On a visit to England

We are the living people of this land, just like the trees and the animals. People from South America, Brazil, Argentina, Peru, Guatemala, those people are praying through ceremony to keep this land alive. They lead a simple life, and they are now speaking out for what is happening.... Trees can't speak, rocks can't speak, rivers, springs, animals, and birds can't speak, so those living people finally have to speak out.... We need to clean up the mess that we created.

If we don't, Mother Earth is going to shake us real hard.

> — THOMAS BANYACYA
> Hopi representative

Brothers and Sisters: We are alarmed at the evidence that is before us.... The people who plant the lands that we have occupied for thousands of years display no love for the life of this place.... We point out to you the Spiritual Path of Righteousness and Reason. We bring to your thoughts and minds that right-minded human beings seek to promote above all else the life of all things.

> — PASSAGES FROM SIX NATIONS IROQUOIS CONFEDERACY
> Statement to the World, May 1979

The land has never been merchandise for us, as it is with capitalism, but it is the support for our cultural universe.

> — JULIO CARDUÑO
> Mexican Indian

To change the land around us is not unlike removing us from the land.

> — GUUJAAW
> Haida Nation, Queen Charlotte Islands
> Off the coast of British Columbia, Canada

What I mean is that — just like us — there are a lot of things that happen inside of Mother Earth. The white man wants part of her insides, which will eventually kill our Mother.... My grandfather told me that coal is like the liver, and uranium is both the heart and the lungs of Mother Earth. She's been living on these minerals underneath the surface of our land.... They are trying to take her precious guts out for money. People are told they can dig here and get rich. But we are even making the air sick with all these smokestacks, and the spills are flushing into our spring water....It's mighty hard to follow the white man's laws....

— ROBERTA BLACKGOAT
Dineh (Navajo), Northern Canada

I need the help of your people to cure sickness. But concerning nature, I need to help your people. The Americans, the English, the Japanese — we want to teach their children and grandchildren not to destroy the earth anymore. The situation isn't dangerous just for the Yanomamis but for everyone. We all live on the same planet.

— DAVI KOPENAWA
Yanomami Indian, Amazon

In our Ainu way of thinking, we take and use the minimum amount for necessities. The Ainu think that it's nature that conserves human beings, not the other way around. If we recognize the limits of nature and live within them, then nature will renew itself.

— SHIRO KAYANO
Ainu, island of Hokkaido, Japan

Our resources came from the land because that makes us part of the land. It's a source of food that is created by that given area; that's what makes my life. Thirty thousand years of legends have been passed on orally as a teaching tool to maintain our existence on how we can live off this land. And how to maintain it is to make sure we do not disturb the resources.

— DAVID B. ANDERSEN
Gwich'in Athabaskan, eastern interior, Alaska

I encourage people to consider Thomas Banyacya's four words: "Stop, consider, change, and correct." Stop what you are doing. Consider the effects of what you are doing. Is it upholding life on this land? Or is it destructive to the life on this land? If it is destructive, then change your value system and your actions. We are not supposed to be subduing the earth, treading it underfoot, vanquishing the earth and all its life. We are supposed to be taking care of this land and the life upon it. So it's up to you to consider which side you are going to be on.

— CRAIG CARPENTER
Mohawk Tribe

The land is our culture. If we were to lose this land, there would be no culture, no soul.

— KUNA ELDER
Panama

ANIMAL WONDER

The first thing a newborn baby touches outside the womb is the deerskin in which it is wrapped by the midwife. A dead man is also wrapped in deerskins. And between these first and last encounters, a person lives with the deer and thanks to the deer.

— ANDREI GOLOVNEV
Nenet reindeer herder
Yamal Peninsula, western Siberia

A fundamental difference between our culture and Eskimo culture, which can be felt even today in certain situations, is that we have irrevocably separated ourselves from the world that animals occupy. We have turned all animals and elements of the natural world into objects. We manipulate them to serve the complicated ends of our destiny. Eskimos do not grasp this separation easily and have difficulty imagining themselves entirely removed from the world of animals. For many of them, to make this separation is analogous to cutting oneself off from light or water. It is hard to imagine how to do it....A most confusing aspect of Western culture for Eskimos to grasp is our depersonalization of relationships with the human and animal members of our communities.

— BARRY LOPEZ
Arctic Dreams

Among my people it is believed that all animals and plants are smart. They can be a friend if you are good.

— DOMANO HETAKA
Brazilian Indian, western Amazon basin

First I took the job breaking horses. I was pretty good at it because I have a lot of patience. I knew that whenever you take a horse from his home you'd better watch the animal closely because the first chance he gets he's going to take off for his home ground. But when I brought in a new horse, I'd corral him with the other horses. Of course, the other horses wouldn't like the new one; they'd try to bite him and push him aside. But I talked to the new horse, "You stay around here. This is your home now, and you and I are going to work together. I will teach you something, friend, and you'll be able to use what I teach you in your life. They'll like you for that, so stick around." And then I'd turn him loose. None of my horses ever took off; they stayed right with me.

— PETE CATCHES
Lakota elder, Oglala holy man

The training of a buz kashi horse is rigid. It begins, in fact, before he is born: His mother gets ten or more eggs a day, to ensure that her foal will be strong. Upon the day of his birth, the colt is prevented from falling to the ground, for that would "destroy his wings." Until he is three years old, he is left to run free.

— SABRINA AND ROLAND MICHAEL
"Bold Horseman of the Steppes,"
On the horses of the Turkoman, nomads of northern Afghanistan

At rest a dog sled is a collection of quarrelsome animals, tangled harness, and wooden boards held together by pegs. In motion, under a man like Johannes, it becomes a thing of beauty, seemingly a single living creature, delicately adjusting pace and direction to the ice conditions ahead.

— JOHN J. PUTMAN
"Greenland Feels the Winds of Change"
On a Greenland Eskimo

Sometimes three moons we travelled, just five of us, tracking one rhino. He knows we follow him. He has strong "dream wanderer." Very difficult. . . . He hears our soft feet on the ground from many rivers behind him. I look in his dirt and talk to him. Tell him where to go, so we corner him. "You need more bamboo shoots," I tell him. "You love them. Head east, O Rhino, to the bamboo forest at the end of the Deng gorge." Or: "River roots, Rhino, so sweet, so tender — go back a bit, for a week or so, towards the trap where the great rivers meet."

— BEREYO
Punan Indian, Sarawak, Borneo, Indonesia

If a hunter is walking in the bush and God wants to, God will tell him, "There's an animal lying dead over there for you to eat." The person is just walking, but soon sees an animal lying dead in the bush. He says, "What killed this? It must have been God wanting to give me a present." Then he skins it and eats it; that's the way he lives. But if God hadn't wanted, even if the hunter had seen many animals, his arrows would never strike them.

— NISA
Kung! woman, Botswana, Kalahari Desert

We never kill for fun, don't hunt on Sunday, and make sure the animals don't suffer. There are rituals for capture and slaughter. After a beaver has been eaten, the bones are given back to the water. Can you imagine how the Crees feel about outside hunters coming up here and killing our food for sport?

— LAWRENCE JIMMIKEN
Cree, Canada

At first I did not see anything until I saw the ears move. It was difficult to see the antlers since he was still in velvet. This was the big moment for me to provide my family with a winter supply of moose meat. Dad showed me where to stand so that I could get a clean shot. I aimed, but did not pull the trigger. Dad looked at me, and I looked at him; I said I wanted him to shoot it. I did not fear the moose or the rifle; my only fear was shooting at the moose and missing it; then my family would not have meat for the winter. It was a question of survival.

— KENNETH JOHNS
Ahtna Indian, Alaska, Copper River

The hunt is never for sport. It's serious, like a ceremony. It's a sacred thing. If you hunt for sport, next thing you know it turns into a war.

— MASANEA
Kickapoo, northern Mexico
Nacimiento de los Kickapoo

I never kill a bird or other animal without feeling bad inside. All true hunters must have that feeling that prevents them from killing just for killing's sake. There's no fun in just destroying life, and the Great Spirit puts that shadow in your heart when you destroy his creatures.

— JOE FRIDAY
Cree, Canada

Some people say that animals are ignorant, but in many ways they're really smarter than us. You don't see a dog trying to be an eagle. You don't see a squirrel trying to be a wolf. The same with the plants. In our language, there is no word for "weed." This word implies something useless, and all of the plants have been given specific instructions from the Creator on what to do. Plants and animals follow their instructions. It's the human beings who don't follow theirs.

— VERNON HARPER
Northern Cree, Canada

The water snake, yellowbelly, that one is lightning. Now the file snake...the file snake you find in fresh water. It can float, and go "tshhhhhhh!" And make the rain. Now a man can make the sound of the snake, and that brings the rain. He will stay home and sleep, and it will start pouring and pouring.

— JIMMY BURINYILA
Aboriginal, Arnhem Land
Northern Territory, Australia

Do you know why the Fulani light a fire for their cows at night? I will tell you. A long time ago, before they owned cows, a Fulani was sitting next to a fire beside a river. A cow came out of the water and as soon as she saw the flames ran back into it. She returned the next day, but the Fulani and his fire were still there, and she fled once more. She was coming out to give birth and, some days later, instead of running back into the water, she lost consciousness. When she came to, she saw her calf and, crouching against it, the Fulani. Thinking them both her offspring, she licked them equally, and from that time the Fulani live with zebus and every night light for them a fire.

— BAMO
Bororo nomad, Niger, Africa

They say if you look at a camel from a certain angle, the curve spells Allah in Arabic.

— ABULWAHAB AHMED
Kenyan Somali, Garissa, Kenya

The health of our people is the health of the herd.

— FAITH GEMMILL
Gwich'in, Arctic Village, Alaska
On the rite of hunting caribou

THE SEER
of BEYOND

MAGICAL LIVING

In the very earliest time, when both people and animals lived on earth…that was the time when words were like magic. The human mind had mysterious powers. A word spoken by chance might have strange consequences. It would suddenly come alive and what people wanted to happen could happen. Nobody could explain this: That's the way it was.

— NETSILIK ESKIMO
Canada

One must relate the origin of the medicine; otherwise, it cannot work its magic.

— SAYING OF THE NA-KHI
Tibetan people of southeastern China

Nothing is really impossible if you know how to control the mind. In the cold you can remain warm, and in the heat stay cool. You can communicate over great distances, and I will teach you how not to feel tired when walking. Would you like to walk so fast that you almost fly?

— GEWA KARMAPA LAMA
Tibetan, China

The dolls are particularly close to my heart. My husband used to have to go way out somewhere to collect the buffalo grass for me. After he died, I didn't know what I was going to do to get it myself. Then it started growing in my own front yard.

— LORENE DRYWATER
Cherokee, on crafting her buffalo grass dolls

We believe in magic. The principle of magic is to try. No matter how hopeless our lives appear to be, if we try we take the first step on the path to solving our problems, that's magic. That's the magic my grandmother taught me. She was the last of the Boto people. There are a few of us left who carry some of the blood, but she was the last real Boto. She left me this magic.

— MIGUEL SOTO
Costa Rican Indian, Costa Rica

Yes, I believe in a force which we call Sila and which is not to be explained in simple terms, a powerful spirit, the sustainer of the Universe, the weather — indeed, of the whole of earthly life, so vast that his speech to men is not couched in ordinary words but in storms, falls of snow, showers of rain, tempestuous seas and all the forces of which men stand in awe. But he has yet another way of manifesting himself, in sunshine, calm seas or little, innocently playing children who understand nothing....No one has ever seen Sila. His abode is so mysterious that it is at once near us and infinitely far away.

— NAJAGNEQ
Eskimo shaman, Greenland

Rice is the embodiment of Dewi Sri, the rice mother, goddess of life and fertility. This is a symbolic way for our bodies to absorb the life force she gives us.

— BALINESE VILLAGER
Bali, Indonesia

When I was a child, I learned that the moon was the goddess Dewi Ratih. Then Neil Armstrong landed on it. I still look up at night and pray to Dewi Ratih.

— SURADNYA
Balinese artisan, Indonesia

You know that time before the sun comes up, when the moon is a fish again, swimming in the ocean? That is the time, our ancestors tell us when Barnambirr, the Morning Star, is released from her dilly bag on the faraway island of Baralku. Behind that Morning Star trails a feathered string, tying her to her home, holding Barnambirr low in the sky. See, here comes the sun. Barnambirr must come down now to rest in her dilly bag for the day, just as it was in the Dreamtime.

— BININUWUY
Aboriginal clan elder
Central Arnhem Land, Northern Territory, Australia

By the position of the morning star, P'katieny informed me his people could predict if their small children would stay healthy or when it would rain. To which I countered with a truth just as fantastic: Pointing to the shining lunar disk, I mentioned that the Americans had gone to the moon. Displaying no surprise, P'katieny simply said, "Then there aren't any Americans left on the ground."

— ELIZABETH L. MEYERHOFF
"The Threatened Ways of Kenya's Pokot People"
Pokot cattle herders, Kenya, East Africa

Once I looked at the moon and caught sight of a strange thing. A cricket had perched upon the handrail, only a few inches away. My line of vision was such that the creature filled the moon like a fossil. It had gone there, I thought, to live and die, for there, of all places, was its small definition made whole and eternal. A warm wind rose up and purled like the longing within me.

> — N. SCOTT MOMADAY
> Kiowa-Cherokee Indian
> *The Way to Rainy Mountain*

My grandmother and my father have told me this story of eclipses. They are caused by Betara Kala, an ugly, giant son of god who was thrown out of heaven. He is trying to eat the sun in his vengeful anger. I know this is not modern thinking. But we think if we make enough noise, we can scare the giant away.

> — ASMO WIYONO
> Native of Patuk, Java, Indonesia

For generations we regarded Muztagata as the highest mountain in the world. Now we know it is not.... My grandfather told me that there is a beautiful garden on top where white-robed saints live in peace and harmony. Please tell me if that is true when you climb the Ice Mountain Father.

> — TURDI BEG
> Kirgiz, mountain nomads of China
> Muztagata: 24,757' in the Chinese Pamirs
> Speaking to American skiers

What causes earthquakes? All Japan is a land of earthquakes. Hokkaido, the land of the Ainu, has always had its share of them. An earthquake occurs when a chiraichep, a big fish that lives underground, wiggles its tail. Immediately after a tremor is felt, an ekashi [an elder] sticks a sword or, if he has none, a knife, in upright position into a corner of the fireplace, threatening the fish with such words as these: "If you don't stop wiggling your tail, I will thrust this knife through your backbone." And with this he pushes the knife farther down. This done, the earthquake ends.

— TAKEICHI MORITAKE
Ainu poet of Japan, Hokkaido

If you have ears for them, the forest is full of sounds — exciting, mysterious, mournful, joyful....At night, in the honey season, you hear a weird, long-drawn-out, soulful cry high up in the trees. It seems to go on and on, and you wonder what kind of creature can cry for so long without taking breath. The people of the forest say it is the chameleon, telling them that there is honey nearby. Scientists will tell you that chameleons are unable to make any such sound. But the forest people of faraway Ceylon [Sri Lanka] also know the song of the chameleon.

— COLIN M. TURNBULL
Dweller among the Mbuti
Ituri Forest, Democratic Republic of Congo, Africa

We Zuni believe our beloved ones, when they are dead, return as clouds — in summer rain, in winter snow. I saw this beautiful purplish cloud with white-silver trimming. And I said to myself, "Hey, maybe you're my mother, and you visit me on my birthday." I had tears in my eyes ... and I knelt on the hard floor and asked the Man Upstairs to give her a place of peace.... Spirits are always with us to help us make right choices.

— ALEX SEOWTEWA
Zuni in New Mexico

I was invited to participate in a funeral ritual for a local woman.... What struck me most was the electric sewing machine. Learning from a neighbor at the memorial altar that the machine was likewise destined for life in the Realm of the Polar Star, I pointed out that it would obviously be useless there, since in heaven there are no electric outlets. . . . I asked one old man why they decided to bury it also. "Several years ago," he answered, "the husband of this old woman crossed over to that same place. In this life he was an active man and headed our community soviet. Thanks to his energy and industriousness, we obtained a power station and lights for our dwellings. I do not think that all these years the husband has been in the Realm of the Polar Star, he has been sitting with folded hands, doing nothing. So do not be skeptical: The deceased will have somewhere to plug in her sewing machine."

— YURI RYTKHEU

"People of the Long Spring," writing about his own people
The Chukchis of the Russian Arctic

The rainbow is the shape of a great doorway, opening, perhaps, to some world we still do not know. But it is so far away that no one has to be afraid of the lovely-colored light in the sky.

— NETSILIK ESKIMO
Canada

Earth itself hovers loose in the air.

— ESKIMO SAYING

A CERTAIN SENSIBILITY

Before there were wristwatches, we used to tell time through an internal timepiece. We always knew exactly when to meet for work in the fields or forest. Now that there are watches to tell us the time, everyone's internal timepieces have fallen into disrepair.

— VISHNU MAYA
Gurung tribe, central Nepal

Time. Yes, time. Is time real? Or merely an illusion, something man has fashioned to measure his progress in a timeless universe? In one's inner self, time takes a different form. Not flowing like a river but calm like a lake. Have you noticed, for instance, that in dreams, past, present, and future blend freely?

— SAFER DAL
Sufi, Yemen

Life is a great white stone. You, a child, stare at it and see only one side. You walk slowly around it. You see other sides, each different in shape and pattern, rough or smooth. You are confused; you forget that it is the same great white stone. But finally you have walked around it, stare at all of it at once from the hillside above. Verdad! Then you see it: how it has many different sides and shapes and patterns, some smooth, some rough, but still the one great white stone: how all these sides merge into one another, indistinguishable: the past into the present, the present into the future, the future again into the past. Hola! They are all the same. With wisdom who knows one from the other? There is no time, which is but an illusion for imperfect eyes. There is only the complete, rounded moment, which contains all.

— MARIA DEL VALLE
Herb woman
Sangre de Cristo mountains, New Mexico

That is my mother, who pays minute attention to the events around her, particularly those which concern her and her family. I used to ask her what time of day I was born. "Oh, I remember exactly," she said. "It was just the time when our oxen and buffaloes were coming in from the field." Clocks and watches were nonexistent in her world then. Time was, and still is to a great extent, measured by rain, harvest, the roosters' crow, the movement of the oxen and buffaloes.

— KOSON SRISANG
Thailand

Not in my head, everything about me knows. Knowing it is like the river that comes out of the ground here and flows as the land slopes. Soon it will join another river and then another until it gets to the ocean. The river knows the earth and the river knows the river it joins. There's no confusion, just a knowing that the source of all the rivers is the same.

— MASANEA
Kickapoo, northern Mexico
Nacimiento de los Kickapoo

I am amazed at how easily the herders sort out their own animals, since none has marks of ownership. "I recognize my sheep as you would recognize your children," says Nanda Lal. "I do not have 150 children," I reply. "Yes, but you recognize people of your village by the way they eat, walk, or talk. So it is with my sheep."

— ERIC VALLI
"Himalayan Caravans"
Speaking to a Rong-pa sheep herder of Central Nepal

These women can visualize a complicated pattern when they weave a rug. They're able to memorize circuit designs in the same way.

— PAUL DRISCOLL
Manager of a semiconductor plant
On Navajo women workers, Kayenta, Arizona

When I asked my friend Bawi Bafki how many children she had, she paused. Then she began naming them, concluding, "Oh, and Wida. Is that six? No, wait, seven." She beamed: "I have seven children." Her initial uncertainty reminded me how irrelevant counting is to the Bahinemos. Bawi's world is not governed by numbers or schedules. Some things are constant: the sun, the rain, the incessant spread of vegetation. Others happen unpredictably: children, wild game, thunderstorms, malaria, love, death.

— EDIE BAKER
"Return to Hunstein Forest"
Papua New Guinea

We Sioux believe that there is something within us that controls us, something like a second person almost. We call it "nagi," what other people might call soul, spirit or essence. One can't see it, feel it or taste it, but that time on the hill — and only that once — I knew it was there inside of me. Then I felt the power surge through me like a flood. I cannot describe it, but it filled all of me.

— JOHN (FIRE) LAME DEER
Lakota

I was to find star-compass techniques still practiced over much of the Pacific. I was even more impressed, however, by the island navigators' uncanny ability to steer by wave motion — swells reflected from islands beyond the horizon.... Almost literally he "steers by the seat of his pants" — sensing the ocean swells through the scrotum.

— DAVID LEWIS
"Wind, Wave, Star, and Bird: Isles of the Pacific"
Navigators of Polynesia

After 35 years in the field, Kamoya Kimeu still displays an uncanny knack for spotting fossils. His 1984 discovery of a Homo erectus skull fragment led to the recovery of a nearly complete 1.6-million-year-old skeleton.... Kimeu sometimes imagines that the fossils speak to him from the stones and rubble, revealing the secrets of our oldest kin.

— MEAVE LEAKEY
Anthropologist, on an Ethiopian native

We Punans know we have two souls. There's the physical, emotional soul, this [smacks his forehead with the palm of his hand] and the "dream wanderer." In sleep and special trance, the dream wanderer travels, sees with different eyes, sees pathway of wild animals or lost people.

— BEREYO
Punan Indian
Sarawak, Borneo, Indonesia

I can feel the life of the fiber. I can hear it. Perhaps we respond because of our own veins and arteries. We are knitted and connected, like the fiber. So often today people don't even think about paper. They just throw it away.

— KYOKO IBE
Artist in Kyoto, Japan
On "washi," handmade paper

We Indians can see and hear with our minds.

— IGNACIO
Makuna Indian, eastern Colombia, South America

LIFE AND DEATH

All that exists, lives.

— CHUKCHEE SHAMAN
Siberia

You are a vessel, just a vehicle and a human being. That's why it's really very important to live as closely as you can to the life that was here before this society. And yes, it's difficult, but not unreachable. When you establish that great faith, you can go anywhere and communicate and adapt.

— ROSE AUGER
Woodland Cree, Canada

Do you know what the soul really is? It is the primitive in us.... Some people sneer at us. They think we are advocating a return to the idea of the Noble Savage! They are incapable of understanding! We do not want to "return" to anything; we only want to peel off the layers of paint and varnish, chrome and plastic behind which we human beings have hidden ourselves from ourselves, and so come to the true man buried underneath.

— YOUNG SIBERIAN MAN
From Shelekhov region near Irkutsk

Ya can't see life, ya know. It's a man you see movin' you call life.

— CARL GAYLE
Rastafarian, Jamaica

Hold on to what is good, even if it's a handful of earth. Hold on to what you believe, even if it's a tree that stands by itself. Hold on to what you must do, even if it's a long way from here. Hold on to your life, even if it's easier to let go. Hold on to my hand, even if I've gone away from you.

— PUEBLO PRAYER
American Southwest

I don't know why we die. I don't know why we live. Sometimes it seems I know nothing.

— MASARANI
Boat-dwelling Bajau of the Tawitawi Islands, Philippines

One of the first things our elders taught us was that when the time of purification comes a big mirror will be brought in. We will be judged in front of the mirror, and it will reveal your judgment. Now I would say that it may be like a computer. They will ask you a question and check your answer against the years of information that are stored in it.

— MARTIN GASHWESEOMA
Hopi elder

A human being's disease is not just what you can see physically, but the sum of his whole life.

— OVE ROSING OLSEN
Inuit, Greenland

We are going to clown our way through life making believe that we know everything and when the time comes, possibly no one will be prepared after all to enter the next world.

— EMORY SEKAQUAPTEWA
Hopi

O you who rest in this place, we come to tell you that tomorrow, when the Eye of Day is half along its course, we will take you and lead you to the Land of Ancestors, where you will lie forever with your family. Therefore, be not absently gazing at yourself in the spring, nor captive to the charms of the valley; be at the meeting-place upon the hour.

— SOOTHSAYER
Before the tomb of a departed Malagasy villager, Madagascar

Today would be a perfect day to die — not too hot, not too cool. A day to leave something of yourself behind, to let it linger. A day for a holy man to come to the end of his trail. A happy man with many friends. Other days are not so good. They are for selfish, lonesome men, having a hard time leaving this earth.

— JOHN (FIRE) LAME DEER
Sioux medicine man

TRUTH IN WISDOM

To ignorance, wisdom is frightening....We must all learn to be unafraid of the dark, the child of learning, the man of wisdom. Hence we shall all reach the true maturity which is eternal youth.

— MARIA DEL VALLE
Valley dweller near Sangre de Cristo mountains, New Mexico

To truly know a thing, one must live it completely. Through the body. When the body has learned, so has the heart, the inner parts of your being.

— CHEA HETAKA
Brazilian Indian, western Amazon basin

The truth always prevails, no matter how many years it may take. So when a person lives in honesty and truth, you never have any real hardships because truth is like a medicine, and it's always going to take care of you. No matter how much you get persecuted.

— ROSE AUGER
Woodland Cree, Canada

A man of truth and conviction, she said, was like a rooster who can crow from the top of a trash heap as well as from the top of a castle.... More important than one's word of honor or the word of an Englishman was the word of Ernesto, and once I gave it, I had to keep it, regardless of how much it hurt.

— ERNESTO GALARZA
Barrio Boy
Jalcocotán, mountain village in western Mexico
On his mother's influence

Truth may walk through the world unarmed.

— BEDOUIN PROVERB

All true wisdom is only to be learned far from the dwellings of men, out in the great solitudes and is only to be attained through suffering. Privation and suffering are the only things that can open the mind of man to those things which are hidden from others.

— IGJUGARJUK, ESKIMO
Noatak settlement, Alaska

The truth can be only one way when there is an oath taken.

— AMAR KHAN
Kurd tribal leader, Iran

He looked upon us as sophisticated children — smart but not wise. We knew many things and much that is false. He knew nature, which is always true. His were the qualities of character that last forever. He was kind; he had courage and self-restraint, and though all had been taken from him, there was no bitterness in his heart. His soul was that of a child, his mind that of a philosopher.

— DR. S. T. POPE
Ishi's closest friend, in *Ishi: Last of the Yahi tribe*
On Ishi, who wandered into a farm yard in Oroville, California in 1911

Just like the two wings of a bird must be balanced for it to fly, so one cannot attain enlightenment unless wisdom is accompanied by compassion.

— LADAKHI MONK
N.E. Kashmir, Indian-Tibetan border

When I was young, an old sage told me that if I never learned how to read and write, and my soul remained unburdened with worldly learning, then I would flower into my destiny and live out my time.

— GUSTI NYOMAN LEMPAD
Balinese artist, teacher

As long as there is ignorance, there is a need for ritual. It is a ladder that may be discarded once we have attained a certain level of spiritual development.

— HEAD LAMA OF STAKNA MONASTERY
Ladakhi, N.E. Kashmir, Indian-Tibetan border

The only thing to ask for when you pray is wisdom, ask to be granted wisdom, then you won't have to worry about the rest. Ask how to live and get by with what you have and to treat the other people like you want to be treated. If you treat other people like you want to be treated, you'll forget about your pocketbook, you'll forget about what you're going to eat tomorrow, you'll forget about what you're going to wear tomorrow, it won't worry you. You'll forget all your worries. That's what life is all about.

— WILLARD RHOADES
Achumawi band, Pit River tribe

Most important truth of all is hardest to see because man of today will not be brave enough to look. Man, wolf, caribou, walrus, snowbird...all are one. Each day man moving farther away from truth into bowels of iron world. Spurning natural world with hard boots and smashing truth and hopes for life. We try to understand true way, Anatoly and me. We living only for that truth, and telling of it for all men!

— EDVARD GUNCHENKO
Descendant of ancient Yukaghir, Siberia

The most precious jewel you can have is wisdom.

— BHADRA MARAPANA
Ratnapura gemologist, Sri Lanka

THE HEARTWEAVER
of RELATIONSHIP

LOVE'S TOUCH

We Dolgans live on our fair earth, with love we warm the ground.
. . . So plant this seed of peace and love throughout the whole wide
world, then keep it warm with hope and trust.

— OGDO AKSYONOVA
Dolgan, Arctic

Please! Sit here by the stove. It gives a good warmth — just as you.

— TSURUKICHI SEKI
Ainu, island of Hokkaido, Japan,
Inviting a guest into his home

When one's heart is glad, he gives away gifts. It was given to us by
our Creator to be our way of doing things, we who are Indians. The
potlatch was given to us to be our way of expressing joy.

— AGNES ALFRED
Kwakiutl, British Columbia, Canada

Everybody jump up and hug up.

— WILLIE REDHEAD
Grenada native

One afternoon during a visit to a neighboring village we observed a most unusual practice: a group of about fifty young women (and some of their children) had formed a circle around a single older woman. They were dressing the happy woman in colorful beads and cloth and singing to her. They paraded her through the village, chanting a beautiful chorus to her.... After a few more songs and cheers and a brief dance from the delighted older woman, the group quietly disbanded and all went back to their respective huts, their soft laughter trailing as they slowly disappeared. When we inquired about this ceremony, we were told that from time to time the young and middle-aged women of the village select an older woman who is single or widowed and pay her a special tribute by decorating her in bright colors, parading her throughout the villages, and singing songs to her that say she is still beautiful and still loved by the people of the village. These compassionate, so-called primitive people seemed in many ways so much more advanced than many of their counterparts in the United States.

— S. ALLEN COUNTER
I Sought My Brother
On the Bush African-Americans in the interior of Surinam
South America

I am convinced that every person has agreeable and disagreeable characteristics, and I look for the agreeable ones!

— AINU WOMAN
Rankoshi, Hokkaido, Japan

I will not be involved with the dreams of angry men.

— HMONG VILLAGER
Laos

Chi choen — "What's the point?"

— LADAKHI SAYING TO DEFUSE ANGER
N.E. Kashmir, Indian-Tibetan border

When people become entrenched in their positions as enemies, the danger is that they can no longer think of any other form of existence. It has happened in Northern Ireland. It is also happening to Afrikaners. We have lost our faculty of compassion.

— BEYERS NAUDÉ
Afrikaner, South Africa

I heard the voices of my ancestors crying to me in a voice of love, "My grandson, my grandson, restrain your anger; think of the living; rescue them from the fire and the knife."

— KIOSATON
Iroquois

I want our people to let go of their hate. We've been pushed around so much. Battered this way and that. But it's not our way to feel hatred in our hearts. Or the greed that even some of our own people have today. That's not the Indian way to be. My dream is to let the greed and hate go and bring back the old ways.

— MARIE SMITH
Eyak Indian, Cordova, Alaska

To the Mbuti, the past is unimportant because it is gone completely and forever. As for the future, they have little desire to control what does not yet exist. The present is something that happens every day and is to be enjoyed with consideration for others, with love, and sometimes with passion.

— KEVIN DUFFY
Children of the Forest
On the Mbuti of the Ituri Forest
Democratic Republic of Congo, Africa

Carefully observe what way your heart draws you, and then choose that way with all your strength.

— HASSIDIC SAYING

With a stout heart, a mouse can lift an elephant.

— TIBETAN PROVERB

The Nyinba have no word for "love." They call it "beautiful from the heart."

— DAVID MAYBURY-LEWIS
Millennium: Tribal Wisdom and the Modern World
On the Nyinba of Nepal

Ladakhis experience the world through what they call their "semba," best translated as a cross between "heart" and "mind."

— HELENA NORBERG-HODGE
Ancient Futures
On the Ladakhis in the Himalayan region of Kashmir

The source of good lies in our hearts, and the heart, by itself, is worth three times more than talent.

— NGUGYN DU
From the poem "Kim Van Kieu," Vietnam

Love is the one true reality — without it all the wonderful things men are doing will mean no more than words of regret carved on a tombstone.

— LYDIA GORSHKOV
Tchersky, Siberia

Hold your son close in your arms, love him well for the blood in his veins. Hold him close, oh, my son, for you hold your wife too in your arms.

— APUTNA
Inuit, Hudson Bay, Canada
Speaking to her son-in-law whose wife has died

Whenever we are gathered together, even if there are only two, and we are speaking with an open heart and a good mind in order to create an understanding, we sit in a circle. Because there are always the Unseen that have gathered there with us. Once you get up from this circle, you will never be the same individual that you were when you sat down. We have sat and shared the vibrations and the energy that have traveled the circle in us and through us. Our hearts and minds have been opened; that's the law that our people knew and practiced. That was their way of teaching.

— SARA SMITH
Mohawk Tribe, Iroquois Confederacy

Give me a man any time who does good to me because he loves me rather than one who does good to me in order to fulfill his moral duty....

— TAN TAI WEI
Singapore

Yes, I knew what he meant, and I knew that for God's sake he wanted to touch me too and he couldn't; for his eyes had been blinded by years in the dark. And I thought it was a pity, for if men never touch each other, they'll hurt each other one day. And it was a pity he was blind and couldn't touch me, for black men don't touch white men anymore, only by accident, when they make something like "Mother and Child"...I wanted to touch him, but I was thinking about the train. He said "good-night" and I said it too. We each saluted the other. What he was thinking, God knows, but I was thinking he was like a man trying to run a race in iron shoes and not understanding why he cannot move.

— EDWARD SIMELANE
South African native
Lamenting how a white man, while taken with his sculpture
"African Mother and Child," could not show his emotions

Would that you had come yesterday, then God would have let us be friends longer.

— HAMID
Rashida tribesman, Ethiopia
Meeting someone for the first time

Everything adds up to a four-letter word — love.

— NOBLE SAMUEL
Native of St. John, Virgin Islands

No exchange of anything except love.

— DANNY DAFLA
Native of Eritrea, Africa

LOVE'S HOLD

There must be love before love-making. But in Russia it is possible to fall in love in one minute...if only both people will allow themselves to do it.

— CHUKCHEE WOMAN
Russia

When I was a girl, some of the young men thought I was beautiful and called me Shamandura, which is a light that shines on the river at night to guide the boats. I was married at 15, and the wedding lasted 15 days. On the second night my husband and I went to the Nile at four o'clock in the morning and washed each other's face with the water from the river.

— GRANDMOTHER HAMIDA
Nubian villager, Egypt

My people are of the tundra, and I wish to be among them. I dream one day of meeting someone who will be my subject of love. The tundra is wide and one must look far, but in time I will find him.

— VERA ETYNKEU
Young woman, east Russian Arctic

The only way to tell if a Burmese woman is married is by her behavior. She wears no ring, and she keeps her own name and property. By law and custom, Burmese women are equal. We couldn't have one law for women and another for men, could we?

— U SAN WIN
Burmese, Myanmar (formerly Burma)

See the two bottles sitting on top of the chimney? That homeowner has two daughters ready for marriage. But see *that* one — a broken bottle? A widow or divorcee lives there. It is like advertising.

— NERMIN ERKAN
Port of Alanya, Turkey

My first six wives were all wonderful women, but this present wife is an angry woman, and I have aged at least ten years since marrying her. If a man has a good and kind wife, he can easily live 100 years.

— ONE-HUNDRED-YEAR-OLD AZERBAIJANI
Caucasus Mountains, Russia

If the crops aren't good, you lose only one year. If your wife isn't good, you lose a whole lifetime.

— HMONG SAYING
Laos

Why do you talk like that, saying you take care of your heart while I take care of mine? When people marry, when I married you, your heart became mine and my heart became yours. I don't want you telling me now that your heart belongs only to you and mine, only to me.

— BESA
Kung! man, Botswana, Kalahari Desert speaking to his wife Nisa

It's easy to make children, but it's not so easy to feed them, you know, with those things of the heart.

— JOHN AUGUSTINE
Native of Vieille Case, Dominica

I had many loves then.... When I run into one of them these days, at the store or on the road, I say to myself: Here comes that old scarecrow, that girl I used to make love to. Now she calls me an old buzzard and uses me to scare her grandchildren. They are white-haired and some have faces all wrinkled like walnuts, faces land-scaped like the Badlands. But I imagine I still see that twinkle in their eyes. That never dies.

— JOHN (FIRE) LAME DEER
Lakota

Once there was a woman, and it was she who was my belly and my blood. Now she waits for me in that distant place where the deer are as many as the stars. She was Kala, and she was of the Sea People, and not my People who lived far from the sea on the great plains where no trees grow. But I loved her beyond all things in the sea or on the land. ...I loved her for the son she had borne, for the clothes that she made me, for the help that she gave me...but it went beyond that. I do not know how to explain it, but Kala held me in her soul. The love she gave me passed far beyond respect for a husband and entered that country of pleasure which we of the People do not often know.... While I live I shall take gifts to her spirit each spring.

— ANOTEELIK
Inuit, Hudson Bay, Canada

A man and woman stay together until their hair is all white.

> — BALAYEM
> Tasaday cliff dweller of Mindanao, Philippines

The restrictions which the Romanies [Gypsies] put on sex relations are like the jetties and levees raised beside a river to keep it from overflowing, and which have the effect of causing the current to flow more deeply and more swiftly.

> — IRVING BROWN
> *Gypsy Fires in America*

I want you to love life more because of me.

> — ROMA SAYING

I bade you farewell, wished you a journey full of blessing. Every hour you exist, when you go to sleep and when you keep in mind the troth between us. I am waiting for you. Come safely back, come safely back.

> — SOMALI NOMADS
> Ogaden Desert, Africa, to a separated lover

Aloha oe — "My love to you."

> — POLYNESIAN GREETING

THE EMBRACER
of HUMANITY

OPEN OPTIONS

Please try to fathom our great desire to survive in a way somewhat different than yours.

— YUP'IK ELDER
Village of Nightmute, Alaska

You must realize our mode of thought is not your mode. Europeans often ignore this truth. We have survived for a long time in a world where survival was very difficult, and we learned how to do it. When the blizzard lashes the taiga, only a fool tries to face it and struggle with its power. But only a fool abandons himself to it and lets it blow him where it will. The wise man leans against it and lets it push him slowly, slowly, so he can pick his path and find his way to safety. This is what we are doing.

— SIMEON DANIELOV
Yakut in Siberia

We do not wish to do anything contrary to the will of the Great Spirit.... We think if the Great Spirit had wished us to be like the whites, he would have made us so. We believe he would be displeased with us to try and make ourselves different from what he thought good. I have nothing more to say. This is what we think. If we change our minds, we will let you know.

— DAYKAURAY
Winnebago Indian

It is generally believed that white men have quite the same minds as small children. They are easily angered, and when they cannot get their will they are moody and, like children, have the strangest ideas and fancies.

— POLAR ESKIMO

In our language there is no word to say, "I'm sorry." That's why a knowledgeable Indian will often not say too much, and some white folks might mistake this for being dumb. But we were taught not to speak too quickly unless we're sure of what we're saying because words can be like weapons, they can hurt. The white man has lots of words for "I'm sorry."

— SONNY BILLIE
Seminole Medicine Man, Florida

When the Creator first made people, they were all equal. But "sumAsaui" (beneficial spirit) told the Creator that people could not be equal because no one would know how beautiful, poor, strong, or intelligent they were, so they must be made unequal. So the Creator made the differences that exist between men, and he sends these as fortune to each of us when we are born here.

— ASENEAE
Sensuron, Borneo, Indonesia

We laugh at a failure — at a slip of the tongue, at someone who stumbles clumsily where grace is required; the Iatmul people of New Guinea, on the other hand, laugh uproariously when a child or a foreigner gets something *right*.

— MARGARET MEAD
Anthropologist, *Some Personal Views*

It is not always that we want a point in our stories, if only they are amusing. It is only the white men that want a reason and an explanation of everything; and so our old men say that we should treat white men as children who always want their own way. If not, they become angry and scold.

— NETSIT
Yukaghir, Siberia

Do you really eat chickens and fish? I am sure that you could not do such a revolting thing!

— TSARANG LAMA
Speaking to an American visitor
Mustang, Nepali-Tibetan border

In the Kazakh tradition the most venerated guest, generally an older man, carves the sheep's head and serves pieces weighty with symbolism. The ears go to children so they will be more attentive. The palate is served to teachers to make them more gentle with students.

— MARIA KENDRO
Peace Corps volunteer in Kazakhstan, Russia

If you want to know what development means to us, you must be willing to accept that our mode of development is not the same as yours. Our development is not based on accumulation of material goods, nor on the greatest rates of profit, obtained at the expense of our territories and future generations....For us, development must take into account the future of an entire people.

— EVARISTO NUGKUAG
Brazilian Indian, Amazon Basin

God damn a potato!

— WASHAKIE
Shoshone
In response to the pressure to become a truck farmer
to exist in a changing world

All we ask is to be permitted to be ourselves, live our lives, determine our own fate.

— YVETTE OOPA
Polynesian villager, Huahine, Polynesia

We have to articulate what we mean by change, define what we perceive as essential to our way of life. We have to refuse to accept blindly others' perceptions of progress.

— PATRICIA LOCKE
Lakota Indian

The Gypsies [Romani] represent an exceptional case: They are the unique example of an ethnic whole perfectly defined, which, through space and time for more than one thousand years, and beyond the frontiers of Europe, has achieved success in a gigantic migration — without ever having consented to any alteration as regards the originality and singleness of their race.

— JEAN-PAUL CLERBERT
The Gypsies

The biggest danger is wanting to live like everybody else.

— PACHANOS
Cree, Quebec, Canada

A NATURAL BLEND

Our people are growing gently into the twentieth century. They are adapting to it without much strain in the same way all living things can adapt to change when it does not come upon them too abruptly or with too much violence.

— SIMEON DANIELOV
Yakut in Siberia

We are a happy people. We don't ask too much of others. We just want to go steady and slow.

— TORE LOKOLOKO
Papua New Guinea

Kale phé — "Take it easy — go slowly."

— TIBETAN SAYING

We walk on two legs, Indian and Occidental. Sometimes we stumble but, more and more, we march at a steadier pace.

— DAVID VELA
Guatemalan

Lhamo khyong, Lhamo khyong. Yale khyong, Lhamo-le — "Make it easy. Easy does it."

— LADAKHI SAYING
N.E. Kashmir, Indian-Tibetan border

Change is inevitable, and change is important. Sometimes you get that uncomfortable feeling that you can't change anything. There is always somebody around saying you have to do things the old way; the old ceremonies are dying, you have to hang on, you have to be traditional. The fact is, there is always change and our people have always been comfortable with it. Change is important when you have to make do with what you have.

— JOE DAVID
Haida Nation, Alaska

Innovation is important. I see tradition a continuous process. While we are alive and have still got years and years ahead of us, and will have grandchildren behind us, what are we going to leave them? A few little bits and pieces of what the anthropologists wrote down? We've got the ability to see where our people are at. Why shouldn't we create new things? We seem to get stuck with that word "tradition." Who is to define what tradition is? People say, "Oh, that's not traditional." So what is tradition? Is it something that has a lid on it, and nothing else can be put into that bucket?

— DOROTHY GRANT
Haida Nation, Alaska

We're not afraid of change. But to see our people shopping in their own center, to see our timber industry go from a struggling business to what it is today, to make our own mistakes and not have the BIA

155

some other agency make them, and then to learn — this feels good. This is Apache identity!

— RONNIE LUPE
Apache, Fort Apache Reservation, Arizona

We want to preserve our identity and take our place in society according to our worth.

— RAJKO DJURIC
Romani, England

We must start thinking like Hmong Americans. Take the best of Laos and the best of America and live like that, but stop thinking like refugees.

— KOU YANG
Hmong native living in the United States

My son has his own path. He already knows Lego! But he doesn't make helicopters or cars. He makes temple gates and funeral towers. Every generation re-creates its culture.

— SURADNYA
Balinese artisan, Indonesia

We mix up our Indian regalia and customs a lot. But we've still got our old ways.

— THOMAS MUSKRAT
Cherokee

We must learn to adapt.... For the sake of our souls we must never forget our heritage. Meanwhile, to survive this life, we better learn to live with the rest of Australia.

— KEN COLBUNG
Aboriginal, Gnangara Lake, Australia

My youngest one here, you can't say he's losing it, because he likes what I do, but he also likes what's happening on the other side. So I tell him there is nothing wrong with living in two worlds. Absolutely nothing. You can come back here and switch a switch and do what you want here, but you need to maintain the principles that have been established — maintain those and keep those. Don't try to fix what has been established for thousands of years by our elders. I tell him if you try to change that perspective you'll have problems.

— DAVID B. ANDERSEN
Gwich'in Athabaskan, Alaska, eastern interior

We try to teach our Indian children . . . you are Indians, therefore, you should realize you are Indians, nothing else but Indians. Think like Indians, be like Indians, but learn English, learn how to write, be educated. You are Indian, you have other ideas. Be educated. You have somebody else's mind. You have two minds and you can work with both. You can have three languages, if you want, or two. . . . We do not want to lose out on being Indians.

— BUFFALO TIGER
Miccosukee Indian, Florida

I used to think that reading and writing were something magic, something for people of high birth. Now I can sign my own name instead of using my thumbprint, and I can read the numbers on the bus. I feel part of a larger world.

— TIRUWORK YILMA
Ethiopian villager, Africa

Education is the ladder. Tell our people to take it.

— MANUELITO
Navajo tribal leader

I've become a planner. I keep an inventory of each day. Maybe the things I plan are illusions, but I see progress all around me, in places I least expect it. I see it in the way the kids today are more aware than we were. They speak up for themselves. My generation was taught to keep our mouths shut. I tell my kids, "When you see me doing something wrong, tell me — I'm only human."

— ALICIA VÁSQUEZ
Born in the village of Pan de Azúcar
Colombian Andes, South America

We have a saying: "From anything old a new sapling must grow."

— VERONIKA GOLIÁNOVA
Slovak, Slovak Socialist Republic

We hold to our ways so we will know who we are and to help us feel good about our existence upon the earth. We do not reject the modern technological world. We reach for it to improve the quality of our lives and to create a secure environment where we can safely pursue our Apache ways.

— RONNIE LUPE
Apache, Fort Apache Reservation, Arizona

I was nine when my grandfather took me to Tutuila and I saw my first car. "What's that," I asked him, "a large pig?" From here to Tutuila was a big step.

— CHIEF TAUILI'ILI
Living on tiny island of Ofu, Samoa

Nobody expects to go back to the way we used to live, but we can have parts of it — caribou, char, bake-apple berries, salmon — that's all we need.

— FRAN WILLIAMS
Inuit from Nain, Labrador, Canada

We need to find a way for all of us to walk in two worlds at once, to be a part of the world culture without sacrificing the cultural heritage of our own families and traditions. At the same time we need to find ways to allow other people to walk in two worlds, or perhaps even to walk in four or five worlds at once.

— JACK WEATHERFORD
Savages and Civilization — Who Will Survive?

A woodcarver gave me one of the Mansaka household gods, made only for the homes of the tribesmen. He said simply, "Now, on your way, take our god so he will guide you back to your place."

— KENNETH MACLEISH
"Help for Philippine Tribes in Trouble"
Eastern Mindanao, Philippines

We hope you will find the right road, backward and forward.

— ZULU ELDER
Speaking to Zulu youth about their changing world
South Africa

Even though you and I are in different boats — you in your boat and we in our canoe — we share the same river of life.

— OREN LYONS
Faithkeeper of the Onondaga Nation of the Haudenosaunee
(Iroquois Confederacy of Nations)

UNTO ONE ANOTHER

Love one another, and do not strive for another's undoing. Even as you desire good treatment, so render it.

— HANDSOME LAKE
Seneca

He who thinks only of himself is not respected.

— IVAN HOTYCH
Highlander, Kryvorivnya, southwestern Ukraine

I have felt deeply, even if the knowledge came to me rather late, that we live only through other lives that touch us and that to live in this way at all requires more care than most people are prepared to give. For ultimately there is nothing more astonishing, more fraught with mystery, than the mutual response that occurs across so many obstacles of time, of place, of background, and of the events that form us. When I have experienced it, it has seemed like the only security I have known.

— KENNETH E. READ
Social anthropologist

Islam says that your neighbor is not just the person who lives next door. A neighbor is anyone living in the 40 houses nearest to yours.

— GAD AL-HAD ALI GAD AL-HAQ
Egyptian

I told my cousin Palti that peace would come to this land. Because if one Arab and one Jew can be friends, there's hope for all of us.

— MUSTAFA ZUABI
Arab, village of Dahi, northern Israel

I'm not a rich man according to most human reckonings, but I am rich in ability and I am rich in knowledge; I'm rich in favors, and I'm rich in cooperation with others.

— WEYEWAN ELDER
Sumba, Indonesia

I help my neighbor, and my neighbor helps me. This is the way it has been here since ancient times.

— IVAN HOTYCH
Highlander, Kryvorivnya, southwestern Ukraine

I was thinking in Gwich'in about how to tell you what I was born into. In my language, the closest thing I can come to what you are taking about is — we would say "T'ee teraa'in." It means — how do I explain it — people working together and sharing to accomplish something, "to accomplish common goals." Working to catch fish, working to get birds, working to get rabbit or something, working together to prepare and cook these foods — "T'ee teraa'in."

— DAVID B. ANDERSEN
Gwich'in Athabaskan, eastern Alaska

The Dalai Lama has said that his true religion is kindness. Look at our prayers; they always emphasize concern for others.

— TASHI RABGYAS
Ladakhi, N.E. Kashmir, Indian-Tibet border

Cry for the eye that has cried for you, and feel merciful for the heart that has felt for you.

— PROVERB
Gabra nomads of the Chalbi Desert, northern Kenya

All human beings are born free and equal in dignity and rights. They are endowed with reason and conscience and should act towards one another in a spirit of brotherhood.

— ARTICLE I
Eleanor Roosevelt's International Bill of Human Rights

All my life I suffered, but I always did it selfishly. But when I use the lodge, I do it unselfishly. I crawl in there, and I think about my brothers and sisters. I think about the environment, and I suffer and pray in there.... Our people have always considered the unborn generation in their decision making. We ask ourselves, "How is something going to affect our children?"

— VERNON HARPER
Northern Cree, Canada

When I think about the battle, what comes to mind is that all those people, on both sides, had loved ones.

— HECTOR KNOWSHISGUN, JR.
On the battle at Little Bighorn
Where his Cheyenne forebears fought with Custer, Seventh Cavalry

We need to go back to being people who think in terms of the needs of others. Learn to be kind in the Maori way, be grateful for what you have instead of asking for too much. Notice when your neighbor feels pain, sorrow, sickness . . . we have to try to rebalance things.

— ELLEMAIN EMERY
Maori islander, New Zealand

In Xocempich one found no classes. The poor were not striving to climb into the middle class, and the middle class did not yearn to get a toehold on the upper crust. All men were essentially equal. To be sure, Don Isidro Pech had more cornfields than poor Valentin. Yet their ways of living were identical. They met on terms of absolute equality, for both were workers. When Valentin got into trouble, Don Isidro would help him; and Valentin has been known to help Don Isidro. Is it not so that freedom comes from self-help and mutual aid, rather than rivalry and jealous conquest?

— LAWRENCE DAME
Yucatan

Without help from others, no one can carry on, either in times of joy or in times of sorrow.

— IVAN HOTYCH
Highlander, Kryvorivnya, southwestern Ukraine

The Ceylonese are happiest with a stranger in their streets or a visitor on their doorstep.

— CEYLONESE SAYING
Sri Lanka (formerly Ceylon)

It's our custom to exchange. We exchange favors and we exchange meat and we exchange labor — how else could it be? You offer me

one hundred people, or I offer you two hundred people in support
— in this way we exchange labor; and this, after all, is the only way
we can reach our goals.

— WEYEWAN ELDER
Sumba, Indonesia

Hands that give also receive.

— ECUADORIAN PROVERB

It is not fitting for a guest to leave my land without refreshment.

— CYPRIOTE SHEEPHERDER
Cyprus

Traditionally, the value of money and the concept of "me" are foreign to our people. We have always done things as a group and
thought in terms of the tribe and the family. I wish the world would
stop a minute and, like the man on the hill watching for caribou, see
what is really happening.

— LINCOLN TRITT
Gwich'in, Northernmost Indians of North America

We know, of course, that our high hopes and pure intentions may
fall flat. But we do know, that insofar as we breathe, we will do our
very best to follow our conviction, in faith and hope. For we have
seen that life is worth living only when it is free and compassionate.
A personal view, of course, but one that sustains us.

— KOSON SRISANG
Thailand

It is all right. We are all here. There is no such thing as alone.

— SAYING OF THE RABARI
Livestock-breeding, semi-nomadic people, northwest India

Corimágua — "I am your friend."

— WAURÁ INDIANS
Brazil, Amazon forest, upper Xingu region

We do not wish to conquer or opress. Nor indeed do we wish to retaliate for two centuries of injustice. Rather we seek to create a new partnership based upon understanding, cooperation, and goodwill. The past cannot be changed: our future is in our hands. Share with us a partnership based upon proper knowledge and understanding of each other's culture and heritage and an awareness of the forces that have shaped the indigenous experience. Share with us a partnership to care for the land which nurtures us.

— LOIS O'DONOGHUE
Yankuntjatjara (Aborigine), northern South Australia

ONE PEOPLE

In the Mayan language, we say, "In laakech," which means "I am you," and we are answered with the words "A laaken," which means "You are me." This is our salutation to one another.

— DAVID BURGOS
Mayan Indian, Muna, Yucatan

The great beautiful thing I learned from the Lakota people is "mitakuye oyasin": all my relations. When they say that, the way it was explained to me, it's so beautiful. It's so immense because it includes everyone who was ever born, or even unborn, in the universe, all the two-legged, the four-legged, birds, animals, rocks, and everyone who's here today. The trees, plants, mountains, sun, moon, stars, and everyone who ever *will* be born! How immense can a statement be? All my relations. I marvel at the beauty of that word; it's so powerful.

— JANET MCCLOUD
Tulalip tribe, Washington state

The Mother Goddess had decreed that "all is oneness" and "many must become one." Everything corresponded to everything: the infinitely small was nothing but the replica of the infinitely great, which itself was a reflection of the infinitely small. Thus the mountain peaks resembled the conical roofs of the temples built by men ... and harmony reigned.

> — KOGI TRIBE
> "The Law of the Mother Goddess"
> Colombia, South America

All who live under the sun are plaited together like one big mat.

> — MALAGASY PROVERB
> Island of Madagascar

We are the beautiful colors of the flowers in the Creator's garden. God loves all the colors.

> — PETE CATCHES
> Hopi Indian

There are different kinds of people in the world. First there are black people; they raise cattle and crops and have their own kind of medicine, which is based on sorcery. Then there are white people, and these people have trucks, and motor vehicles, and they have their own kind of medicine, which is contained in sharp needles. Then there are the red people, us bushmen; we don't have truck or cattle, but we have the mongongo nut, but we also have our own kind of medicine and that is the kind of healing I do. And so you see these are the different kinds of people with the different ways of life, but inside we are all the same. The blood that is inside our bodies is the same color ... we are really one people.

> — KUNG! DOCTOR, 80 YEARS OLD
> Kalahari Desert, Africa

Though I am different from you, we were born involved in one another.

— WHITE-HORSE TIBETAN SAYING

Abundance and scarcity are never far apart; the rich and the poor frequent the same house.

— SOMALI SAYING
Africa

I have a red skin, but my grandfather was a white man. What does it matter? It is not the color of the skin that makes me good or bad.

— WHITE SHIELD
Arikara Chief, South Dakota

We may come in on different ships, but we're in the same boat now.

— WORDS FROM 20TH-CENTURY FOLK SONG "SAME BOAT NOW"

The idea is, "If you allow me to do what I want, I'll allow you to do what you want." You need some cleverness, but when everybody's clever, it's a damn mess.

— BIANCAMARIA FENZI
Anthropologist from Pisa
On the independence of the Neapolitans from Naples, Italy

We call it "ubuntu, botho." It means the essence of being human. You know when it is there and when it is absent. It speaks about humanness, gentleness, hospitality, putting yourself out on the behalf of others, being vulnerable. It recognizes that my humanity is bound up in yours, for we can only be human together.

— ARCHBISHOP DESMOND TUTU
South Africa

Being international opens our hearts.

> — PAULISTANA
> São Paulo, Brazil

It is our Desire that we and you should be as one Heart, one Mind, and one Body, thus becoming one People, entertaining a mutual Love and Regard for each other, to be preserved firm and entire, not only between you and us, but between your Children, and our Children, to all succeeding Generations.

> — KANICKHUNGO
> Iroquois, New York

We're all ethnics together. Who can afford to discriminate?

> — PORTUGUESE VILLAGER

Philip Deer spoke to the Elders Council after he had just come from Europe and Africa, and he had one of these beaded sacred hoops about ten inches in diameter with the four directions in the middle. He laid it down in front of us and asked, "Can anyone tell me where this came from?" We passed it around and looked at it. Somebody said, "It looks Arapaho to me because of the peyote stitch here." Another person said, "It looks like a Southern Cheyenne because these beads come only from a certain period." Everybody had their own ideas about which particular tribe it had come from. He stunned us all when he said it came from Africa. It had the four colors of mankind on it.

> — MIKE HANEY
> Lakota/Seminole

Cultures are many, though man is one.

> — WALTER GOLDSCHMIDT
> Anthropologist, *Ways of Mankind*, 1954

The peoples of Nigeria have welcomed me with one voice, and I hope that this may help you to feel a greater unity among yourselves.

— QUEEN ELIZABETH
Visit of Nigeria in 1956

All people are the same...we come from one line because the earth is round.

— MARIA VÁSQUEZ
Colombian Indian, South America
Speaking to her daughter

When we make offerings to the gods, when we sacrifice our animals, we pray for the world. We pray for everyone — the Japanese, the Chinese, the Mexicans, the Americans, even the Europeans. We must keep praying or the world will stop. We pray to balance the world.

— HUICHOL INDIAN
Sierra Madre Occidental, central Mexico

There is no difference in God, just like all people are equal, God is equal, too. Everyone goes to only one place.

— CLEMENTINA MARTINEZ
Cabecar, Costa Rica

Thlowk toon ewa coosim — "We are all the same."

— YAKIMA INDIAN
Tenet of their traditional faith

In America, the most modern people eat something they call stone-ground wholemeal bread. It's just like our traditional bread, but there it's much more expensive than white bread. People over there are building their houses out of natural materials, just like ours. It's usually the poor who live in concrete houses. And the trend is to dress in clothes with labels saying "100% natural" and "pure wool." The poor people wear polyester clothes. It's not what I expected at all. So much that is modern in America is similar to traditional Ladakh.

From the drama *Ladakh, Look Before You Leap*
N.E. Kashmir, Indian-Tibetan border

Harambee — "Let us all pull together."

— KENYA'S NATIONAL MOTTO

We aim to achieve, through our traditional values, the development and realization of a society in which all peoples can live together in dignity. In the Ainu language, we have a word, "Ureshipamoshiri," which signifies our concept of the world as an interrelated community of all living things.

— GIICHI NOMURA
Ainu, northern island of Hokkaido, Japan

THE WELL-WISHER
of ALL

GRACIOUS LIVING

My grandfather taught me that life is a gift; it was blessed to you.

— ALEX SEOWTEWA
Zuni, New Mexico

Blessings. Blessings be well. Blessings on the cattle. Blessings on the people. Blessings on the homestead. Blessings on the camp. Blessings on the grain. Blessings on the sheep and goats. Blessings on tomorrow, also. And again blessings. Blessings forever.

— KARIMOJONG GREETING
Cattle-herding society, northern Uganda

Life is the ceremony. It is lived every minute of every day. Because of that, there is no word in Cabecar for ceremony. It cannot be put into a word that could explain it.

— TOMAS
Cabecar Indian, Costa Rica

Vannakkam — "May you be blessed with the gift of a long life."

— TAMIL-SPEAKING PEOPLE IN SRI LANKA

Be well, grow old, become wealthy with stock, become an elder, be made wise.

> — ELDER'S WORDS
> During rites of passage for a young male
> Karimojong tribe, a cattle-herding society in northern Uganda

When the time came for me to leave the Wodaabe, Mokao asked me to share with him the traditional three glasses of tea: The first "strong like life," the second "sweet like love," the third, "subtle like friendship."

> — CAROL BECKWITH
> "People of the Taboo"
> On the Wodaabe of Niger

May God make milk for you.

> — SOMALI SAYING
> Africa

I will be happy forever, nothing will hinder me. I walk with beauty before me, I walk with beauty behind me, I walk with beauty below me, I walk with beauty above me, I walk with beauty around me, my words will be beautiful.

> — NAVAJO BEAUTY-WAY

Gan Tanee Gan Gadu — "Thank you, Great God."

> — BUSH AFRICAN-AMERICANS
> Surinam, South America

Everyone must have charm and beauty. Men show their beauty in the dances. Women show their beauty by their displays of calabashes [gourd containers] and the many beautiful things they put on them.

We seek beauty everywhere. It is the Wodaabe Way — grace and elegance in all things.

— JARO
Fifteen-year-old Wodaabe woman
Niger, Africa

Yei a-weh, shtoo-gah xut ya tee — That is the way in which I am thankful.

— WILLIAM PAUL SR.
Tlingit Indian, Southeastern Alaska

Our people never . . . said, "Thank-you." Instead they would say, "I am very happy from my heart for what you have done."

— VERBENA GREENE
Warm Springs Indian Reservation

To the modern way of thinking, I have been negligent . . . in not writing letters of thanks for the kindnesses shown; but early on, when I began to know the languages, I heard Native people making fun of Outsiders because they said "thank you" so often when talk is cheap. If you really want to thank someone, you must "do" something that shows appreciation. . . .

— LAEL MORGAN
Editor, *Alaska's Native People*

I want to drink to women all over the world . . . for them not to work too hard and to be happy in their families.

— KHFAF LASURIA
One-hundred-thirty-one-year-old Abkhazian
Kutol, Caucasus Mountains, Russia

As women, we have a very special privilege and responsibility here on this earth, to bring forth life and to nurture it in its very beginnings. We should respect ourselves for that. It's a very, very high position, and it's sad that a lot of women don't feel that and carry that self-esteem. We don't have to go beyond our means to be equal to men, which is how we differ from so many feminist organizations.

— AUDREY SHENANDOAH
Eagle Clan Mother, Onondaga Nation

I and I give thanks for this that you give... cool runnings.

— TONY COLE
Rastafarian, Jamaica
Double "I" referring to both God and the human,
who live together in each person

Esker Ona — "Thanks with all good heart."

— BASQUE SAYING

To the sea that nourishes us, to the forest that protects us, we present our grateful thanks. You are two mothers that nourish the same child.

— SALUTATION OF TRIBAL PEOPLE
Ainu, island of Hokkaido, Japan

Look, it is obvious that we have a very easy life. The grass grows by itself, the animals reproduce by themselves, they give milk and meat without our doing anything. So how can you say our way of life is hard?

— NOMAD OF CHANG TANG
Tibet

You mean, everyone isn't as happy as we are?

— TSERING DOLMA
Ladakhi, N.E. Kashmir, Indian-Tibet border

We can make a good life if there is no more war. All we need is peace and rain.

— ERITREAN MAN
Eritrea, Horn of Africa

There is always enough, and enough is plenty.

— GUILLERMO
Native of Balearic Islands, Spain

Ny riaka no valamparihiko — "The sea is the limit of my rice field."

— MALAGASY SAYING
Madagascar

Whenever the seasons open, I raise my heart in thanks to the Creator for his bounty that this food has come.

— MENINOCK
Yakima Indian

It is good to remember Pacha Mama, Mother Earth, and to thank her for her bounty.

— RUFINO PIZARRO
Aymaran boatman of Titicaca, lake region of Bolivia

When the Indian potter collects clay, she asks the consent of the river-bed and sings its praises for having made something as beautiful as clay. When she fires her pottery, to this day, she still offers songs to the fire so it will not discolor or burst her wares. And, finally, when she paints her pottery, she imprints it with the images that give it life and power — because for an Indian, pottery is something significant, not just a utility but a "being" for which there is as much of a natural order as there is for persons or foxes or trees.

— JAMAKE HIGHWATER
Native American

You may think this strange. Maybe you'll laugh, but we always prayed to what we took. Before cutting down a tree, we'd say, "Forgive us, understand that we need your warmth." That's what my father taught me.

— MARIE SMITH
Eyak Indian, Cordova, Alaska

Before cutting a tree for the planking, we dance beneath it to pay respect for the life of the tree and the lives of the people who have passed beneath it.

— HARSON SHIRO
Palaun, Pacific Islander
Palau, State of Ngaraard

If we didn't do the ceremonies, it wouldn't mean the plants wouldn't bloom that year. It would mean we would stop having that respect and giving that praise. Then we stop having food to eat because we would lose respect and cut down the rain forest, pollute the water, and destroy the balance. That is the real truth behind this message.

— LEANDIS
Mexican healer, northern Mexico

I shall celebrate my life in the world and the world in my life.

— N. SCOTT MOMADAY
Kiowa

Sukhothai is thriving. In the water there are fish; in the fields there is rice ... whoever wants to laugh, does so; whoever wants to sing, does so.

— WORDS CARVED INTO STONE
Sukhothai, Thailand

The stars are hearing, the earth is hearing. The people are hearing — all is well, good, sweet. Then laugh, laugh, laugh.

— TRADITIONAL BLESSING
Pokot people of Kenya, cattleherders, East Africa

Zenda bashi — "May you live long."

— KIRGHIZ CAMELEERS
Wakhan corridor, Afghanistan

I'M GOING NOW

In our language there is no word for good-bye. When you see some-one off, you say, "toksa," meaning "We'll see you."

— ARVOL LOOKING HORSE
Keeper of the Pipe, Lakota

The Pokot word for good-bye also means "thanks."

— ELIZABETH L. MEYERHOFF
"Kenya's Pokot People"
East Africa, cattle-herders

The Inuit have no verbal equivalent for our good-bye. "I am going now," they say. Others reply, "Yes, you are going."

— INUIT OF UMINGMAKTOK
Above the Arctic Circle

Doe vizhdanae — "Till I see you again."

— BULGARIAN GOODBYE

People never believed in telling each other good-bye. They shook hands instead, and said, "I'm going now, and I'll see you again."

— VERBENA GREENE
Warm Springs Indian Reservation

Salam alaikum. — "Peace be on you."

— MARSH DWELLERS' BLESSING
Tigris-Euphrates, Iraq

Ukubusisa — "Bless you."

— ZULU SAYING
South Africa

Slamat djalan, mas — "May your journey be blessed, brother."

— JAVANESE GOODBYE
Java, Indonesia

"The Hand of God on All Roads."

— NIGERIAN SAYING

"Tharro" — May we reach home safely.

— MUSTANG BLESSING
Northern Nepal

Thank you very much for your effort to know us, to recognize us, to understand us, and to listen to us.

— BEMAL BHIKKHU
Buddhist monk
Chakma tribe, Chittagong Hill Tract, Bangladesh

ABOUT THE ART

Based on rock paintings made at Tassili Cave, in the Sahara Desert, Algeria, between 4000 and 2000 B.C.

Based on rock paintings of women walking, Cueva Saltadora, Pyrenees mountains, eastern Spain.

Mayan hieroglyph from temple doorway at Palenque, Mexico. Dates and events were recorded through a system of dots, bars, faces, and hands.

Water or rain god. Iran, ca. 2500 B.C.

Based on Australian Aboriginal stencils in clay, with extensive use of "U" symbols, representing child spirits.

Red cave painting found at Churchill River, Saskatchewan, depicting a buffalo transmitting power to man.

Based on Australian Aboriginal stencils in pipe clay of small (possibly children's) hands.

Based on eight-thousand-year-old sandstone engraving from Oued Mathendous, Libya, of an extinct buffalo.

Based on traditional art of Haida tribe, Pacific Northwest of United States and Canada.

Native Celt design. The Celts populated Western Europe 5,000 or 6,000 years ago and were forced into Britanny, Wales, Scotland, and Ireland.

Based on Austrailian Aboriginal rock painting, Kakadu, Northern Territory, Australia.

Based on embroidered designs on clothing of Huichol tribe, Mexico.

Avanyu, the plumed serpent related to the diety Quetzalcóatl, from a ceremonial dance kilt, pueblo tribe, American Southwest.

Based on rock paintings from a slate grotto, Salt River Valley, Southern Kaoko Veldt, Southwest Africa.

Based on design of Blackfoot tribe, Saskatchewan, Canada.

Based on desiign of Hopi tribe, Tulare, California.

Based on spirit or ghost petroglyphs from the Upper Little Colorado River region in central Arizona.

Based on detail of Tulare or Yokuts basket, California.

Based on textile design from Sivas, Turkey.

Based on quadraped petroglyphs from the Upper Little Colorado River area.

Based on textile designs of indigenous Guatemalan people.

Based on textile design of Huichol tribe, Mexico.

Based on design of Anazazi people, American Southwest.

Based on design of the Sioux tribe, Great Plains of North America.

Geographic Distribution

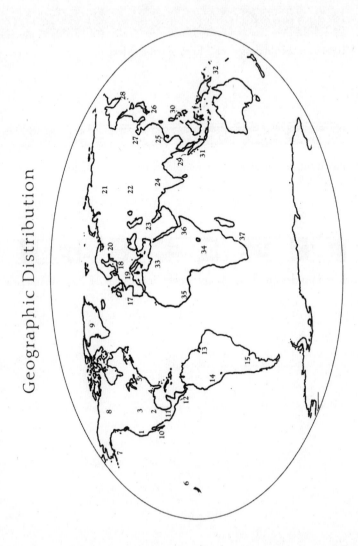

GEOGRAPHIC SURVEY

1. WESTERN UNITED STATES
Colorado: Ute
Arizona: Hopi, Apache, Pueblo, Navajo
Washington: Tulalip, Coeur d'Alene, Yakima, Puget Sound islander
Idaho: Nez Perce
Nevada: Shoshone
California: Yahi, Digger, Achumawi (Pit River Indian), Yurok,
   Pomo, Yuki
Oregon: Warm Springs Indian Reservation
New Mexico: Zuni; Navajo; villager, El Ancon; villager, Sangre de
   Cristo mountains

2. SOUTHCENTRAL UNITED STATES
Missouri: Blackfoot
Arkansas: Cheyenne
Oklahoma: Cherokee (Kiowa), Cherokee Nation

3. NORTHCENTRAL UNITED STATES
Nebraska: Pawnee, Omaha, Winnebago
South Dakota: Sioux (Lakota), Rosebud/Yankton Sioux, Oglal
   Sioux, Lakota/Seminole, Arikara

4. SOUTHEASTERN UNITED STATES
Virginia: Pamunkey
Florida: Seminole, Miccosukee

5. NORTHEASTERN UNITED STATES
New York: Iroquois Confederacy (Mohawk, Seneca, Onondaga
  Nation)

6. HAWAII
Hawaiian native

7. ALASKA
Yupíik, Aleut, Dolgan, Gwich'in, Haida Nation, Tlingit, Eyak,
Yukon native, Eskimo (Noatak settlement, Aleknagik, and Manley
Hot Springs), Ahtna Indian, Savoonga

8. CANADA (HIGH ARCTIC)
Polar Eskimo, Netsilik, Inuit, Dineh, Cree, Blood Indian Reserve,
Labradorian, Kwakiutl, Haida Nation, Micmac, Stoney Indian

9. GREENLAND (HIGH ARCTIC)
Inuit, Eskimo shaman

10. BAJA CALIFORNIA
Natives of El Rosario and La Paz

11. MEXICO
Kickapoo, Huichol, Juchiteca, Mayan, Yucatec, natives of northern
and western Mexico, Aztec descendant, villagers of Mexcaltitán
and Guanajuato

12. CENTRAL AMERICA
Guatemala: Quiche, Guatemalan native, highland villager
Panama: Kuna
Costa Rica: Cabecar, Costa Rican native, Boto
Central America: Garifuna

13. SOUTH AMERICA, NORTHERN COUNTRIES AND
BRAZIL
Brazil: Yanomami, Cinta Largas, Paulistana, Brazilian Indian
    (Western Amazon Basin), Waurá Indian (Amazon Forest),
    Guarani-Kaiowa Indian (southwestern Brazil)
Venezuela: Yanomami, Los Nevados mountain farmer, Goajiro
Colombia: Kogi, Makuna, Goajiro, Colombian Indian, villagers of
    Colombian Andes, U'wa
Surinam: Bush Afro-Americans

14. SOUTH AMERICA, ANDEAN COUNTRIES
Chile: Chilean; villager, Isla Robinson Crusoe
Bolivia: Titicaca native, Aymara
Peru: Quechuan, Aymara (Altiplano Island off coast of Peru)
Ecuador: Jivaro, Ecuadorian villager, proverb

15. SOUTH AMERICA, RIVER PLATE COUNTRIES
Argentina: Gaucho

16. WEST INDIES, CARIBBEAN
Jamaica: Rastafarian
Grenada: native of Grenada
Dominica: native, Vieille Case
Grenadine Islands: Grenadine islander
Virgin Islands (U.S.): Johnian native

17. WESTERN EUROPE
England: Romani (Gypsy)
Wales: native Celt
Belgium: Romani (Gypsy)
Spain: islander, Balearic Islands
    Basque Province, Pyrenees: Basque

Portugal: Portuguese villager
Italy: Neapolitan

18. NORTHCENTRAL EUROPE
Hungary: Roma proverb
Poland: Zakopane artisan, Hassidic saying
Slovak Socialist Republic: Slovakian villagers

19. SOUTHEASTERN EUROPE
Bulgaria: Bulgarian saying

20. BALTIC RUSSIA
Lithuania: Udegei

21. SIBERIA, RUSSIA (HIGH ARCTIC)
Yukaghir; Yakut; Gilyak; Chukchis; Siberian villagers of
River Ob, Chernychevsky, and Tchersky; Shelekhov native;
Nenet of western Siberia; Chukchee shaman

22. RUSSIA
Chukchee; villagers of Azerbaijani, Abkhazia., Kazakhstan, and
Kuibyshevskoye; Hutsul, southern Ukraine; villager, Avdotino;
Roma greeting; Highlander

23. MIDDLE EAST
Saudi Arabia: Arabic saying, Bedouin, Murrah tribe
Turkey: villager, port of Alanya
Yemen: Sufi
Iraq: marsh dweller, villager in Qabab
Iran: Kurd
Israel: villager in Dahi
Cyprus: Cypriote sheepherder

24. SOUTH ASIA
Afghanistan: Turkoman, Pushtun tribesmen, Garmsel villager,
    Kirghiz cameleer
Pakistan: Punjabi, Hunza, Kalash
India: Rabari, villager in Nimkhera, Ladakhi (Kashmir), schoolchild
Sri Lanka: Ceylonese, Ratnapuran, Tamil blessing
Nepal: Dolpo cliffdweller, Rong-Pa, Nyinba, Gurung tribe,
    Tsarang, Mustang
Bangladesh: Murung, Chakma
Bhutan: Bhutanese

25. CHINA
Tibetan nomad, nomad of Chang Tang, White-Horse Tibetan,
Na-khi, Kirgiz, proverb

26. SOUTH KOREA
Korean villager

27. MONGOLIA
Mongolian storyteller

28. JAPAN
Ainu, island of Hokkaido; artisan in Kyoto

29. SOUTHEAST ASIA
Thailand: Karen, Thai native
Laos: Hmong
Vietnam: Vietnamese villager, Mnong village elder, Vietnamese poet
Cambodia: Cambodian villager, Cambodian immigrant
Singapore: Singaporean
Malay Peninsula: Semang tribe, Kelabit tribesman
Myanmar (Burma): Burmese native, Karen

30. PHILIPPINES
Mansaka, Tasaday, Bajau, Panamin

31. INDONESIA
Weyewan, Balinese, Javanese, Sumatra native, Punan, Sensuron, Patuk native

32. OCEANIA
New Zealand: Maori
Australia: Aboriginal, Bunjalung, Yankuntjatjara
Papua New Guinea: Bahinemo, Iatmul, West Papuan elder, Papuan
Fiji: Fiji islander, greeting
Samoa: Ofu islander, greeting
Micronesia: Palaun, Ponapean
Polynesia: Polynesian greeting, Polynesian natives
Cook Islands: Rarotongan, villager

33. NORTHERN AFRICA
Egypt: Nubian, Egyptian
Niger: Bororo, Wodaabe, Tuareg
Sudan: Sudanese native
South rim of Sahara: Songhai
Mali: Dogon

34. CENTRAL AFRICA
Democratic Republic of Congo (Zaire): Mbuti (Pygmy), forest
    dweller

35. WESTERN AFRICA
Nigeria: Nigerian drummer
Ivory Coast: Baule descendant
Sierra Leone: Mende

36. EASTERN AFRICA
Ethiopia: Rashida, Ethiopean
Eritrea: Eritrean native
Kenya: Pokot, Gabra, Turkana, Kenyan native, Masai, Somali
Somalia: Somali nomad
Uganda: Karimojong tribe

37. SOUTHERN AFRICA
South Africa: Zulu, Afrikaner, native
Botswana: Kung! (Bushmen)
Madagascar: Malagasy, Malagasy proverb
Lesotho: greeting

AFTERWORD

In a shrinking world made borderless by high-speed communica-
tion, we can now enjoy daily contact with other cultures and the
value systems of people of different visions and expectations. The
challenge remains for us to respect these differences and to celebrate
that diversity. We must strive in every way to encourage the peaceful
coexistence of different traditions and lifestyles. We must all aspire
to create a more open and culturally tolerant society. Whether we
like it or not, cultural diversity typifies the community of the future.
Let us hope that in this next millennium both the traditional and
the modern lifestyle will exuberantly coexist.

Now more than ever, traditional knowledge is threatened from
globalization and from spreading monoculture. With its subtle
power over us, modernity's many faces pose a threat from all sides to
the indigenous peoples of the world. Because we live in the last ves-
tiges of the world's natural resources, we are relentlessly pursued by
all forms of enticement to convert us to other ways of life and to
distract us away from our interest in our land of origin. In our split
moment of distraction, our history and birthright are taken away

from us. Often, it is state governments that blatantly convert Native Customary Rights land (NCR) into logging, mining, and agricultural concessions. It is vital that we maintain our wisdom in the face of these disdainful acts.

Although the wisdom of the indigenous peoples is rooted in primeval origin, it is both an accumulative and an active cultural experience. It is not the findings of an individual specialist searching through libraries but wisdom learned from our direct contact with the land. Nature's raw elements are truly the source of enlightenment. The discovery of one's infinite links to the universe gives us a sense of being, of rootedness and contentment.

Indigenous knowledge of the natural and spiritual, of animals and their connections to humans, demands in all of us a renewed consciousness that we humans are not separate from other beings. This consciousness of the intricate "web of life" is a positive worldview that can sustain the fragmented world we have created. The modern knowledge we're so excited about is, perhaps, in reality, the masking of our own fear in accepting the infinitesimal and mysterious role we have in the universe. Modernity prides itself in "discovering," controlling, and recreating nature. Instead, we ought to admit humility and return to wholeness once more. There is no knowledge so fresh that nature has not seen it before.

Those of us born in the forest know the forest speaks to us! Nature bears its own spirit. We also know the forest bears the marks of those before us — the spirits of our ancestors, witnessing all we do to the land. Nobody who walks in the jungle can ignore the presence that speaks to our spirit. If we care enough to be sensitive, we can become in tune with the sacred. When we bear such sacred knowledge of the land, we will not accept any part in its decimation. For what are we without the land except prisoners in our steely environments of concrete jungles and sterile landscapes that can't sustain us? What will those following us inherit?

The old peoples advise us that we all must fashion our lives toward becoming role models — models of lives forged in different experiences, lives bathed in great sweat of pain and struggle, lives celebrating gratitude and the simplicity of living. Such life experiences are often borne in the depth of questioning during dark nights and solitude, in living with the harsh reality of precarious seasons and landscapes. This wealth of experiences is summed up in the many traditions and cultures that cross our path every day. It is easy to dismiss or to forget the richness of these other experiences amidst our own biases and preoccupations.

Strong role models provided by parents, grandparents, and society are important to the youth who will inherit our destiny. I am reminded of the majesty and power of the eagles. How do they teach their young to be eagles? How do they manage with no language? They teach by modeling. The young observe the adult soaring above the storms and turbulence that hit the edge of the cliff daily. Such is required of us all. Life isn't only about "do's and don't's," but rather about living a quiet life of example brought about by much wisdom. From wisdom comes the knowledge of balanced living — of living in commune with nature. We all strive for this balance in our lives; it takes the patience of a lifetime.

The book you have here, *Simply Living,* presents life lived by example. The words of wisdom speak about living life daily from a cohesive, global perspective. The editor's effort at weaving together a tapestry of wisdom must be commended, for it brings to us a worldview not presented in the mainstream media. The importance of this knowledge collected and organized in one place is that it shows a positive worldview of wholeness. When we read these powerful words, something ancient and mysterious is awakened in our spirit. It is as if the call of the wild resonates in our being! Indeed, this is how it ought to be, for we are children made of free will — free and wild as nature intended us to be.

The words in *Simply Living* also remind us that the eternal lives in us. The breath that beats silently in our breast is the eternal presence of the Creator of the universe. Often we ignore it. We search for it in the high mountains, in the depth of caves, or through risky adventures, but the restlessness remains. This breath holds our living body together, molding lives, beauty, and compassion with it, connecting us to nature and the eternal universe. It is not ours to possess. We just have to acknowledge its presence, how its linkages connect all of us. These linkages make us one and equal. We are not born one above the other; when it all ends, our physical body belongs at ground level, but our spirit soars into the heavens to renew its connection once more.

It is evident from this global collection that the thoughts are consistent throughout the ages, fluid and flawless, wise and witty. At a glance, *Simply Living* could have easily been mistaken as coming from a single person, a single moment. Of course, that person is none other than *human,* one we meet everyday. No matter what our skin color or social status, or what we have made ourselves into, deep in the crunch of our soul, we are one — *humanity.* Therefore, we all deserve equal respect from each other.

I hope that many books like this one, *Simply Living,* will be written because they challenge the popular notion that traditional knowledge isn't worth pursuing. We cannot let traditional knowledge disappear; its origin is too ancient. Our new knowledge will be much richer with the presence of traditional knowledge.

I applaud Shirley Ann Jones for her initiative and wisdom in collecting these insights and helping us realize that true wisdom does not know age, time, or place.

— MUTANG URUD
Kelabit tribesman, Borneo, Malay Peninsula
Affiliated with Endangered People's Project (EPP)

ABOUT ENDANGERED
PEOPLE'S PROJECT

The EPP acknowledges and celebrates the diversity of human cultures and experiences and strives to maintain and promote this awareness among people. EPP works in collaborative effort with indigenous groups to assist in campaigning for urgent situations or in channeling their messages through books, videos, and lectures. Because we believe in celebrating living cultures rather than disappearing ones, we make exhortations to pursue what we have, and at the same time preserve and record what is left.

A powerful example of the need to maintain awareness is the Penan of Sarawak, one of the last true nomadic groups in the world. Just a decade ago about five hundred were nomadic; now barely two hundred remain. By the end of the century, only seven or ten families may be left to pursue the traditional Penan lifeways.

Shall we long for things only after they're gone, or shall we prevent their disappearance?

ABOUT THE EDITOR

Shirley Ann Jones is rooted in diverse living. She has a degree in biology with a chemistry minor and a master's degree in English, specifically the teaching of writing. She has written books that range in content from the history of barbed wire to the wisdom of science to basics of sex education. As a child, she transferred from a city school in Phoenix, Arizona, (a district large enough to have elementary schools numbered Madison #1, Madison #2) to a country schoolhouse in Pope Valley, California, with grades first through sixth all in one room, with one teacher. Here she lived on a ranch rich with heritage. Indian mounds, remains of an old Wells Fargo station, a two-story Victorian home built in 1885, the valley's historic cemetery were all located on the ranchland. She found delight in the simple and the natural: caring for "bummer" (orphaned) lambs as well as fawns, discovering bright rocks in the creek, fishing in the lake, hiking in the hills, and riding horseback to the neighboring ranch. Later, she married a man who had the very same connection to the land, the son of the man who owned the ranch before her parents bought it in 1954. He migrated on to another part of the country, but time and timing brought them back together. An English/

German heritage from her father and a Scottish/French heritage from her mother, Shirley's descendants include inventors (barbed wire, typewriter, servo valve) and agriculturalists — a blend of the innovative and the practical.

Shirley is a nutrition educator with the University of California Cooperative Extension, teaches a research writing course at the University of the Pacific, with a focus on connecting to the larger design of living, and is currently writing a book entitled *The Little Stranger* about how we find our lessons in life in the most unexpected,out-of-the-ordinary places. Shirley lives with her husband in Lodi, California, and has two grown sons and four grandchildren.

If you enjoyed *Simply Living*, we recommend the following New World Library titles:

Native Heart: An American Indian Odyssey by Gabriel Horn. A deeply moving account of one man's sacred journey as he struggles to live the way of his ancestors in modern America. Gabriel Horn reflects upon his relationship with the Great Mystery, the stars, birds, trees, and Mother Earth. *Native Heart* is a celebration of the great heritage of the Native American people, and moves all of us to consider our own sacred path.

Neither Wolf nor Dog: On Forgotten Roads with an Indian Elder by Kent Nerburn. This winner of the 1995 Minnesota Book Award draws us deep into the world of a Lakota elder indentified only as Dan. With humor, pathos, and insight, we are taken through the myths and stereotypes to the heart of the Native American experience. An unlikely cross between Jack Kerouac and *Black Elk Speaks.*

The Sacred Earth: Writers on Nature and Spirit edited by Jason Gardner. Drawn from the great works of contemporary American nature writing, this profound and beautiful collection of 145 quotations of poetic prose from more than 60 of our finest nature writers celebrates the earth and explores our spiritual relationship with nature.

The Soul of an Indian: And Other Writings from Ohiyesa (Charles Alexander Eastman) edited by Kent Nerburn. Ohiyesa, a Dakota Indian, has been described as "the Native American Thoreau." Also known as Charles Alexander Eastman, Ohiyesa is one of the most incisive and sensitive of Native American thinkers. He writes on the Great Mystery, the "Temple of Nature," the power of silence, the presence of Spirit, poverty and simplicity, nature and solitude, the importance of prayer, the appreciation of beauty, the teaching of children, the moral strength of women, the sacredness of honor, the reality of psychic powers, the meaning of death, and a great deal more. Ohiyesa's voice must be heard.

Welcoming Spirit Home: Ancient African Teachings to Celebrate Children and Community by Sobonfu Somé. Somé's wisdom inspires us to allow our indigenous selves to come alive. We can learn to reawaken the part of us that understands the language of spirit and ritual as well as its deep meaning and healing. And, in so doing, we find that we are able to apply the power, understanding, and sense of completeness we gain from these rituals to our everyday lives. By so doing, our lives become more balanced, more fulfilling, and more complete. We can then expand this knowledge to our communities and gain a much greater sense of purpose and peace.

Wisdom of the Native Americans: Including the Soul of the Indian and Other Writings by Ohiyesa and the Great Speeches of Red Jacket, Chief Joseph, and Chief Seattle edited by Kent Nerburn. The teachings of the Native Americans provide a connection with the land, the environment, and the simple beauties of life. This collection of writings from revered Native Americans offers timeless, meaningful lessons on living and learning.

The Wonders of Solitude edited by Dale Salwak. This volume of quotations on the essential importance of solitude helps bring contemplation and silence back into our busy lives. It contains more than 300 inspiring and diverse quotations on the importance of nature and power of solitude. *The Wonders of Solitude* is an uplifting companion in the struggle to remove ourselves, as Salwak writes, from "our peripheral concerns, from the pressures of a madly active world, and to return to the center where life is sacred — a humble miracle and mystery."

New World Library is dedicated to publishing
books and cassettes that inspire and challenge us
to improve the quality of our lives and our world.

Our books and cassettes are available at bookstores everywhere.
For a complete catalog, contact:

New World Library
14 Pamaron Way
Novato, California 94949

Phone: (415) 884-2100
Fax: (415) 884-2199

Or call toll free: (800) 972-6657
Catalog requests: Ext. 50
Ordering: Ext. 52

E-mail: escort@nwlib.com
http://www.nwlib.com